# Streets of Heaven

# Streets of Heaven

125 years in the parish of St Mary's Bourne Street

## 1874 ~ 1999

edited by Neville Price

St Mary the Virgin
30 Bourne Street
London SW1W 8JJ

First published 1999
by the Church of
St Mary the Virgin
30 Bourne Street
London SW1W 8JJ

© Copyright 1999 the Vicar and Churchwardens of St Mary's Bourne Street.
Introduction and editorial matter Neville Price, 1999.

A CIP catalogue record for this book is available from the British Library.

ISBN 0 9508 516 6 3 (pb)
ISBN 0 9508 516 7 1 (hb)

Designed and typeset in 11 pt Bembo by Michael Boag.
Cover photograph by Audrey Stallard.
Cover design by Richard Poole.
1894 map courtesy of Alan Godfrey Maps.
Printed in Great Britain by Page Brothers (Norwich) Ltd.

*Streets of Heaven*

# Contents                                      Page

# Appendices

# List of Plates

# Foreword

## The Bishop of London

I HAVE ALWAYS LOVED St Mary's Bourne Street. It is a church where I can hear the rich language of Cranmer prayed within all the splendour of the Western Rite—*agnosco veteris vestigia flammæ*. Thanks to a notable succession of faithful and gifted priests, and loyal and prayerful parishioners, the detail of the Liturgy has never overwhelmed the simple commandments of the Christian faith. It is a place of spiritual refreshment for the widest variety of people and I am delighted that memories of St Mary's have been collected for this volume to inspire us for the years that lie ahead.

+Richard Londin:

# Introduction

## *The Editor*

CHURCHES CAN BE FAMOUS for a variety of reasons. Some are famed for their architecture, some for their great age. Others are known for their liturgy, their preachers—even for their eccentricities. It is the privilege of St Mary's Bourne Street to be renowned as a centre of Anglo-Catholic principles and teaching.

Some years ago, when I attended mass at St Mary's for the first time, I was impressed by the ceremonial, the rich vestments, the music and the atmosphere of reverence and holiness. How did this little church, not much bigger than a chapel, come to be here? Why was it so hidden away? Who was responsible for its strong practice of Anglo-Catholicism? When was it built, and by whom?

With these unanswered questions buzzing in my mind, my librarian's instinctive curiosity led me to consider an investigation into the history and times of this lovely church. Later, when I was asked to write a history of St Mary's to celebrate its 125th anniversary, I accepted only with some misgivings. I was conscious of my lack of qualifications for the task and, more so, of the scarcity of available documentation.

In the end I placed my faith in research and set out to produce a book that would balance two elements: history on the one hand, and faith and practice on the other. I also determined that, as far as possible, the contents should be written by the people of St Mary's. The book you now hold has, in its first part, six articles on the continuing and developing life of St Mary's both as a parish church and as part of the Church at large. It looks at the departed priests-in-charge and vicars, all of whom have served us so well. The second part discusses five aspects of St Mary's through articles on our music, vestments, liturgy, publishing history and architecture. The title, *Streets of Heaven*, is taken from a hymn written in 1921 and unique to St Mary's. It is printed in its entirety, with music, in Appendix I.

Our little church was dedicated to St Mary the Virgin on

2nd July, 1874. The building resulted from a decision by the management of St Paul's, Knightsbridge, to build a mission chapel in the poorer section of the parish. The Reverend W Beaumont Hankey—a close friend and adviser of many of the leaders of the Catholic movement—was its first curate and, later, priest-in-charge. In 1909 the district was constituted a separate parish, having for its first vicar the Reverend Cyril Howell, who died in 1916 and was succeeded by Fr Humphrey Whitby.

Fr Whitby and his warden, Lord Halifax, ensured that the Catholic faith was taught and practised fearlessly and intelligently. Indeed, Lord Halifax was involved, between 1921 and 1926, in the Malines Conversations (dialogue between the Roman and Anglican communions). St Mary's was also enlarged under Fr Whitby, with the assistance of the architect, HS Goodhart-Rendel, and of artists such as Martin Travers and Colin Gill. The church and its congregation later survived the wars, seeing the numbers of its men depleted and its children evacuated. When Fr Whitby retired in 1948 he left a solid Catholic foundation on which subsequent priests would build.

In 1974, under Fr John Gilling, the church celebrated its centenary. By then it had witnessed the decisions of the Second Vatican Council in the Roman Church. Later it was to see the historical decision to ordain women as priests in the Anglican. Our diverse and expanding congregation consists of friends from many countries as well as regular 'St Mary's people'. Among the latter is former churchwarden Cicely Paget-Bowman, who has been worshipping here since 1921. The Anglo-Catholic tradition has been fully maintained and, while we preserve our beliefs and our liturgy, its continuance should be assured.

A complete history of St Mary's has yet to be written. This book omits, for example, our church's involvement in the Prayer Book Crisis of 1928 and in the Eucharistic Congresses during the inter-war years. These events are documented elsewhere. Our own researches have taken us to many sources. Among these are the parish magazine, complete from 1874 to the present day. For architectural plans and drawings there is the library of the Royal Institute of

British Architects. Occasionally one discovers a personal reminiscence of many years ago. One such is that of Fr David Powell, a curate in 1936. His memoir is printed here. Personal memories can be created by educated guesswork. There is such an example in this volume. Many genuine memories have, alas, been lost forever.

But *Streets of Heaven* is not an apology for an incomplete history. Rather, it is a tale centred on our church and parish over 125 years, told in 11 contrasting and informative chapters. It has been compiled as an act of gratitude to our founders, benefactors, former priests and earlier congregations. We hope you will value it as such.

I would like to express sincere thanks to my contributors for their great labours of research, all carried out with a publisher's deadline looming and to all who have given their support, especially my friend and church administrator, John Greenhalgh, without whose help this volume would not have been published.

# Part I

# What St Mary's means to me

*Faith and History*

# Those were the days

*Extracts from the Diary of Walter Nye (1874)*

SATURDAY 28TH FEBRUARY. My name is Walter Matthias Nye. Walter after my uncle (2nd Warwickshire) who fell at Chilianwalla in 1849 and is commemorated on the obelisk at Royal Hospital, and Matthias after my saint's day. I am writing this in the book that I was given as a birthday present by my Auntie Georgiana, my date of birth being February 24th in the year of 1858. As any scholar can work out, I am 16 years of age. I am writing this with an extraordinary novelty: the new Letts liquid ink pencil, a present from my Uncle John. He is Auntie Grace's husband. It is a remarkable instrument because the supply of ink is seemingly unlimited and I may carry it in my pocket. From my father I was given five shillings (a fortune!) and from Mam a pocket handkerchief, which I will always treasure.

What I wish to do in this book is to tell a little about myself and my whereabouts. Until my 14th birthday I was a scholar at St Paul's Church School in Wilton Place. Now, of course there are schools at St Barnabas's and St Michael's. At St Paul's, under the edifying, but sometimes furious tutelage of Miss Daunt, I was taught the rudiments of a Christian education, or so my dame told me. These were spelling, arithmetic, religious knowledge and some history, and manners. In addition, once a week, Mr Sandby taught our class drawing. Without boasting, I think I can say that Mr Sandby paid particular exception to my work and drawing is something I still take great pleasure in.

I cannot claim to be a great historian. That is a joke! But Miss Daunt told us about the Romans and the Kings and Queens of England and a little bit about the doings of the common folk, and that is one of my reasons for writing this journal. I myself would be interested to know what folk were doing in my part of Pimlico a 100 years ago, so perhaps a 100 years hence people might be interested in my meagre recollections. So much has happened hereabouts,

---

but that is the way of the world we live in. Nobody alive a 100 years ago would recognise the world we live in today.

Now I will tell you about myself. I stand five foot and four inches and weigh about nine and a half stone. I have brown hair and blue eyes (two arms and two legs—another joke!). My family consists of my father George Nye and my mother Lizzie Nye (née Calthorp), and my two brothers: Philip, James and my two sisters, Ada and Rose. There were three other children, but they were, alas, lost in infancy. My mother comes from Strumpshaw in Norfolk, but if ever I ask my father, who is a Londoner, how he met my mother I am greeted with a wall of silence. We are a very happy family.

We live in Coleshill Street,[1] in the Liberty of the City of Westminster. It is a broad and, I would say, a handsome street of four-storey houses. It is not as grand a place as our aristocratic neighbours in Eaton Square, but nor is it as impoverished as the mean streets to the south west of us. But we are all, rich and poor, part of the Grosvenor Estate and our landlord, the Marquess of Westminster[2] maintains it well and his agents look to it that none of his tenants let their homes become shabby.

Our number is 62. In the basement there is the kitchen and behind the servant's room. For now she is Mollie, aged 15, but as my father says these girls never stay long. He says, "We teach them, they filch them." By they he means the big houses in Eaton Square and Belgrave Square. I can't remember one of the servant girls lasting more than 18 months. I like Mollie, though she is very stupid and can't read or write. Money will no doubt soon draw her away to be her Ladyship's undermaid and we'll have another Mollie.

The rest of the house is parlour (used only for grand occasions and funerals) and back bedroom on the ground floor and four more bedrooms on the upper two floors. Out the back there is a yard, where my mother tries, not very successfully, though she would hate me for saying so, to grow flowers. In the yard we also have a cock (noisy) and a few hens, so we don't lack for eggs. The wash house, with a basin and closet, is at the side. By the front door we have a linnet in a cage who, when the sun shines upon it, sings merrily.

We buy chickweed and bits of turf for the bird from the groundsel man. I am proud to live where I do, it is England's capital and the heart of the British Empire and the greatest city in the world.

Many of the houses in our street are lodging houses, as they are in Ebury Street, and, since coming out of the Army, my father has taken in lodgers. We have two. Miss Charlotte Pritchard, a very nice old lady in her 50s who is an annuitant and lives on the top floor next to my sisters, and on the ground floor Mr Zachariah Watkins, who is a cook and confectioner who works in the West End, and I do not particularly care for. He is rather slovenly and I would not care to eat any of his confections.

There is nobody I admire more than my Dada. He is a real Army man. Before he was invalided out he was Company Sergeant Major in the 57th West Middlesex Regiment of Foot, gloriously known as the "Die Hards". He has travelled the world and seen service in the Crimea at Balaclava, Alma and Inkerman where he was wounded and had to leave the service. I wonder whether my mother nursed him. But he will never say.

My best friend is William Ketteringham who is my age. We were at St Paul's Church School together. He lives opposite at number 51 and he works as an assistant to his father who has a bookshop in Sackville Street in the West End. He and I would like to travel the world. It is not approved of by the parents. I also like his sister Emily. She has blonde hair and blue eyes.

I have not yet decided how to spend my life, but to help my family out I am working for the moment as a stable boy at the Livery Stables in nearby Graham Street West.[3] The owner Mr Meeks is a kind man and allows me to take the occasional time off. What I would like to be is a painter, but my parents tell me this is a pure foolishness. In spite of this my father has allowed me (and is paying for me!) to attend drawing lessons with Mr John Louis Paul, the landscape artist, son of the famous animal painter Mr Joseph Paul.

Dada says I should write something of the political state of affairs. Mr Gladstone's Ministry resigned on February 17th and Mr Disraeli formed his second on February 21st. The Conservatives have swept the board with a majority of about 50. In London alone there are now 19 Conservative members. Dada, however, is none too pleased. Mr A MacDonald and Mr T Burt, the first two Trade Union Members of Parliament have been elected and Dada says that life will never be the same again.

In Westminster our Members of Parliament are Robert Wellesley Grosvenor of 62 Queens Gate and the Lodge, Brackley. His club is the Travellers. The other is William Henry Smith of 24 Hyde Park Street and Greenlands, Henley-on-Thames. His club is the Carlton. I extracted this information from the newspaper, I myself don't think it is very interesting, but others may deem to the contrary.

*Monday 2nd March.* An extraordinary occurrence! My eldest brother Philip, who has been working for the travel agent, Mr Thomas Cook, in London has been asked by him to work in his new office in Paris which opens in April, as an accountant clerk. Mam says we will be celebrating before he leaves. Brother Philip has said that I might visit him in Paris. That would be thunderous indeed. I only hope Dada allows me.

*Wednesday 11th March.* As I was walking to work down Graham Street near the Pineapple Public House,[4] Mr Eyton, a curate from St Paul's came up to me and introduced me to his companion who said: "We don't need introducing, we're old friends." It was none other than Mr Withers who had given me architectural drawing lessons when I was 12 and he was working on the open porch of the tower at St Paul's. "Still drawing, are you young man?" "Doing my best, sir."

Mr Eyton explained that Mr Withers is the architect of the new chapel that is being built here on land given by the Duke where the houses were pulled down for the cut and cover of the Metropolitan and District Line Railway eight years ago. They were here to see how the work was progressing. Mr Eyton then told me that he is to be the curate of the new church and that cometh July we would have a new home to pray in. He is an exceedingly pleasant man and asked me if I played cricket, because he was proposing to set up a side. I told him I was medium, which he misconstrued that I was a medium fast bowler. I hope that I am not put to the test. He also told me that in August there were plans for a church outing to the country. Afterwards I asked where we should play cricket and he replied Battersea Fields, which was stupid of me because I knew that. He enquired whether I could sing and I said no.

*Sunday 15th March.* Not having to work today, it being Sunday, I took a walk over the old wooden bridge to Battersea. There are still a few market gardens growing carrots and melons and lavender and asparagus, (still sold as a Battersea bunch[5]), but the railway lines from the Nine Elms Goods depot and the Southwark and Vauxhall Water Works, what with the attendant building, have spoilt much of what was countryside. Even I can remember looking across the river and seeing nothing but fields all the way to the uplands of Battersea Rise and Lavender Hill. And there are the new factories: Price's Candle Factory, Morgan Crucible, Garton Hill's Glucose Works and the London Gas Works with its three huge gasometers.[6]

On the way back I talked to a didicoi[7] boy who was selling birds' nests in Sloane Square (Mam would not have approved!). He wanted me to buy a complete squirrel's nest with young for 8/-, though he said later I could have it for 6/-. He could also let me have live snakes, lizards and hedgehogs for killing black beetles. This last I was almost prepared to buy because my Mam had been urging me to get her some *Cantharikopho* which advertises that it exterminates all vermin. Including us, I wouldn't wonder! This didicoi told me that regularly every week he supplied Mr Butler's herb shop with moss and the Hôtel de l'Europe in Leicester Square with six dozen frogs, also three dozen for a Frenchman who keeps a cigar shop in Charing Cross.

*Monday 16th March.* The population of London is 3,533,484. The Chelsea Water Works Co. supplies nearly 8,000,000 gallons of water daily, but all of it has to come from upstream beyond Teddington because of the foul state of the water further down.

*Wednesday 18th March.* In our parlour Dada has an inscription on the wall that reads "Caste is a good thing if it's not carried too far. It shuts the door on the pretentious and the vulgar; but it should open the door very wide for exceptional merit. Let brains break through its barriers, and what brains can break through, love may leap over." It is from a play by Mr TW Robertson called "*Caste*."

*Friday 20th March.* I would like to ask Mr Ketteringham if I might take his daughter, Emily, on one of Mr G Brooks' pleasure boats from Paddington to Greenford Green, but am not confident how to put it into words.

*Saturday 21st March.* Went to the Public Baths in Victoria[8] and had a very pleasant second class warm bath for 2d. It was definitely worth the extra penny over the cold. Dada told me that until 1856 the Lord Mayor's Show took place on the river and that was why the platforms were called floats.

*Friday 27th March.* I bumped into Mr Eyton again, to my embarrassment because I was filthy mucky from work. He compounded my embarrassment by asking me if I were a friend of Miss Emily Ketteringham. Like St Peter, I denied all knowledge of her. Then he told me that she was considering going on the August excursion and would I not like to join her on it. I hardly knew what to say, but in the end said yes.

*Saturday 28th March.* Mam asked me if I would do some chores for her and as Philip is soon off to Paris and James is a soldier (in the Blues, much to my Dad's pleasure, he could not abide that not one of his sons had followed his profession) and the girls are still scholars, reluctantly I agreed. So I took the bedclothes down to Mrs Hawkins in Skinner Street to be mangled and then went on to Mr Rodgers in Ebury Street for writing paper and Mr Cross for butter, which he had forgotten to deliver. Mr Cross, for though he is a dairyman, lives in Ebury Street and keeps his cows on land in Battersea. I stopped by at 184 Ebury Street, the St Paul and St Barnabas' Dispensary to pay our subscription and was heartily surprised by Mr Morey, the resident surgeon recognising me. It is a good club to belong to because when you are in ill health you are provided with advice and medicine. It was something of a red letter day, because whom should I see, on taking the long way home, but the great poet Mr Browning paying a visit to Mr Moscheles, the painter, in Sloane Street.

*Thursday 2nd April.* Mam read us of terrible news from the paper. The SS Atlantic, bound for Halifax, having fallen short of coals foundered on Meagher Rock near Sambro. 560 lives were lost. It is sure that the Captain will, at least, be suspended. Dada said he should be ceremoniously drowned at sea. I hope that Dada says things that he sometimes does not actually mean.

*Friday 3rd April.* A great throng standing on the corner of West-bourne Street and Graham Street West[9] all looking heavenwards. I joined them half expecting to witness some sort of miracle, which I suppose in a way it was. There were four men on the spire of the new chapel and with the aid of pulleys and winches they were endeavouring to put a copper weathercock into place on the top. At one moment one of the men lost his hold and slipped and a terrible gasp went up from the crowd. Fortunately he recovered his footing and hauled himself up again. When at last the vane was safely secured we all hollered and clapped like mad and the men waved back at us.

*Sunday 5th April.* "Walter, you are growing up and will soon be a man." Fearful words to hear from a father. We were taking a walk together down the Grosvenor Canal where it runs parallel alongside the railway tracks, under the cranes and up to the swanky new hotel, the Grosvenor. It is a favourite walk of ours after high tea. "Walter, my boy, there are several matters I wish to discuss with you, now that · you are no longer a boy." My heart, as you can imagine, was sinking fast. "I'll begin with the bad and move on to the good. You are an agreeable looking boy, but innocent, I believe, and there are wicked people who would take advantage of you." I saw a heron perched upon a wooden stump in the water and prayed my father's talk would cease. "People you should avoid are the flower sellers. Now many of them are respectable, married women, but there are a minority of others who pay their 1d. rent a day for a basket and to you, with their pretty flowers, their moss roses, their violets, stocks and lily of the valley, they may look like sweet young things. But I am telling you that many a snake lurks in the grass." I didn't truly

*Those were the days*

understand what he meant but he carried on. "And have you heard of the straw sellers?" "No, sir." "Well, these gentlemen will sell you literature that purports to be indecent, but, upon examination you will find that the book you have bought contains nothing but blank pages." "Well, Dada, I cannot see how that could harm me." "Foolish boy, to pay five shillings for a book of empty pages." There were two ships in the canal, one drawn up by the Bangor Slate Wharf, unloading roof tiles for the new buildings across the river, or so I imagined. The other, a ship with a foreign name, was tied up by the Baltic Wharf unloading timber. "And now for the good news. Your brother Philip travels to Paris on Tuesday and tomorrow night we are to have a farewell feast for him and, if you care to, you may invite your young friend Emily to join us." "No, Father, I couldn't." I must have blushed, because I have never felt as hot in my face in my life.

*Monday 6th April.* We had the party for Philip, and a slap-up do it was. First there was a huge sirloin of beef with roast potatoes and carrots and cabbage. After that we had plum tarts and junkets. Ada and Rose had helped Mam with the cooking and Dada had provided us with India Pale Ale to lift our spirits. After dinner Dada announced that once Philip had settled in Paris, he proposed that I should be allowed to travel there to stay with him. He said that he'd already spoken to Mr Strutz, the Swiss courier who lives in Graham Terrace and that he had agreed to accompany me at a convenient date. My joy was unconfined. I only wished that I had had the temerity to invite Emily. She would have been so proud.

William's father will not allow him to join me on my adventure. I think William might have been more insistent.

*Tuesday 7th April.* Philip departed for Paris with much joyful and yet sorrowful weeping from his family. I can't wait to join him.

*Saturday 11th April.* I am paid 4/- a week when my work ends at two o'clock on Saturday afternoon. On my way home this Saturday I bumped into Mr Eyton who was again looking over the building of the chapel. He asked what I thought of it. I told him I thought it very red. He laughed and said: "Well, it would, being made of red bricks. You sound very jangly, are you a rich man?" "No, sir, it's just that I have been paid my wages." "We'll need that for the new chapel." I hope he was just jesting because I have to give Mam 3/- of my earnings. After that he introduced me to the man who was with him, a handsome fair haired man called Mr Hankey, who is to be his colleague. They are to live in Minera Street. They have invited me to tea, which I may well decline, particularly if they are to invite Emily as well.

*Wednesday 15th April.* Dada read out items from the newspaper. There has been a revolt of Herzegovinian peasants against Turkish rule, the Herzogovinians being supported by Bosnia. He might have been talking about the inhabitants of the Moon as far as I could make sense of it. He said I was an ignorant boy. Then he told us that Mr Livingstone's remains, accompanied by his faithful retainers Susi and Chuma had been brought back to London to be deposited in Westminster Abbey. I applaud and understand that. Mr Livingstone was, and is, a hero of the Empire.

After that he poured himself a glass of port wine, in spite of Mam saying: "You know you shouldn't, it's not Christmas after all." Chuckling, he pulled down a book and turned the leaves. "I want to know which of you can tell me which famous author wrote this. 'Cadogan Place is the one slight bend that joins two great extremes; it is the connecting link between the aristocratic pavement of Belgrave Square and the barbarism of Chelsea.' Not a little unlike our own situation I would say." Quick as a flash, Ada responded: "Charles Dickens, Father." "Well done my little girl, I'm proud of you. You are right. It's from *Nicholas Nickleby.*" Yet I knew that my little sister was cheating, because, like it or not, Dada does not have what might be called an extensive library and she must have recognised the volume he had taken down.

*Thursday 16th April.* Wrote to Philip today to confirm my travel arrangements. Wondered whether to send him a letter at a cost of 2$^{1}/_{2}$d, or a postcard at 1$^{1}/_{4}$d. It only takes a day (unlike Canada which takes 11 days) and the mail is made up every morning and every evening. In the end decided on the letter, on the grounds that, even though it is more expensive, it looks better to the recipient. I can hardly wait for next week.

*Sunday 19th April. Easter Day.* Dada asked me if, before I travel to Paris, I would go and visit 'Old Man' Sutherland who is now poorly in the Infirmary at the Royal Hospital. He was a friend of my grandfather, who died seven years ago. They were both in the Scots Guards and fought at Waterloo, which is where my grandfather lost an eye. They were born at the time of the French Revolution which seems a long way back now.

'Old Man' Sutherland was sitting up in bed and looking pretty cheery for an ill man, especially compared to the rest of them in the dormitory. He has a snow white moustache and hair the same. His family were crofters until the Clearances, which was the reason for his joining the Army. "Have you come to bury me, lad?" "No, sir, I'm on my way to Paris to stay with my brother, Philip, and Dada said you could do with a visit." "Aye, so I could too; they're a deadly lot in here, look around you, not a Kiddie here. Did I ever tell you why we are called the Kiddies?" He had, often, but I judged it prudent to be innocent. "Oh, no sir, never." "Well, a little history never hurt anyone. It all goes back to 1686 when King James II made a camp at Hounslow Heath. He wasn't popular and he feared that there might be trouble in London. The Grenadiers were there, and the Coldstreams, and us, and we being the junior Guards regiment were nicknamed the Kiddies. So it's been ever since." I laughed, I hope sincerely, and asked him if there were anything I could bring him back from Paris. "A sweet little Mamsell would be a treat."

*Wednesday 22nd April–Tuesday 28th April.* The great day has arrived! Mam woke me at five, much too early, but I was awake already. After a desultory breakfast, all those of my family still at home came to see me off. As we live so close to Victoria Station Dada judged it improvident to take a cab, so he and I carried my case between us. I thought this was a bit thrifty, as it would only have cost a shilling. But I suppose it wasn't my shilling. I was installed in my carriage with Mr Strutz well before the train departed at 7.40am. When it did I was at the window weeping and waving as if I would never see them again for a twelvemonth. But then I have never been

away from home before. I should, perhaps, record that Dada has paid
for this venture of mine at a cost of £1.19.0 for the return ticket,
which is available for seven days. The journey through the countryside was very beautiful, though I realised from the smuts of soot
I kept getting in my eyes that I had chosen the wrong side of the
carriage.

We reached Dover at 9.25am and sailed away all but ten minutes
later. The crossing was smooth, but as a precaution against possible
sickness (as advised by Mam) I stayed at the stern of the steamer
and watched the receding coast line, the mighty wake of the boat
and the raucous, circling gulls. I thought it wise not to eat the sandwiches Mam had prepared for me yet, just in case.

We docked in Calais at 11.35am and departed for Paris less than
an hour later, reaching Amiens at 3.52pm and Paris, the Northern
Station, at 6.00pm. I must say that I thought the French countryside
through which we passed was not as beautiful as dear old England.
But then I am partisan.

It was a joy to see Philip waiting for me on the platform. He
grabbed hold of my case and, having bade Mr Strutz farewell, we
were soon in a *fiacre*, as they call cabs here, bound for his lodgings
in the Rue Tholozé, beneath the hill of Montmartre, with a windmill up at the end of the road. His lodgings are not exactly capacious,
but we'll get by.

As a treat for my first night in Paris Philip took me to a brasserie
where we both ate chicken in a sauce of vegetables[10] and drank red
wine. We sat at the table talking for hours about family and what we
planned to do with our lives. I felt very happy and most grown-up.
Philip has suggested that as he does not have to work tomorrow
and knowing of my interest in painting we go to an exhibition of
new, young French artists.

The exhibition, entrance fee one franc, was in the famous pho-
tographer Nadar's old studios in the Boulevard des Capucines. It
was a great mixture: some of the paintings seemed very unordered,
slapdash almost, and others gaudily coloured, some seemed mere
impressions. One I liked very much, by A Renoir, was of a lady

in a box at the theatre. The names of the other exhibitors were C Pissarro, C Monet, P Cezanne, A Guillaumin, A Sisley, E de Gas, B Morisot (I liked his[11] works, though they were very wispy), de Nittis, E Boudin and Braquemond. Who knows, one day they may become as famous as Jean François Millet who has just died, though I doubt it.

*Thursday 30th April.* Back in England it seems as if the week I was away in France never happened, just like a dream, though having said that I have inextinguishable memories and the knowledge that Philip and I are now more intimate and close friends, more than just brothers.

*Saturday 2nd May.* Gave 'Old Man' Sutherland a cheap and ugly doll I bought in Paris. He laughed and said I was a "young blade."

*Saturday 16th May.* A great day for our part of London. The Chelsea Embankment is to be opened. Three–quarters of a mile long, it runs from Chelsea Bridge to Albert Bridge, it covers the old open sewer. It took three years to build at a cost of £269,591, so Dada says. I wonder what the £1 was for. I went down for the occasion and by barging my way to the front was able to catch a glimpse of the Duke and Duchess of Edinburgh officially opening it. They looked very grand.

*Monday 8th June.* The lion atop of Northumberland House has been removed. It is to be taken to Sion House at Isleworth. Northumberland House is to be demolished. Rumour has it that the Duke will be recompensed to the tune of £500,000. Dada says that it is quite right and proper. I am not so sure. It seems a large sum of money to give a duke who is already rich.

*Sunday 28th June.* Something melancholy happened to me today. William Ketteringham and I were prying about the nearly finished chapel when Mr Eyton caught sight of us and came over. He took us to the porch and showed us a beautiful stained glass window of the Mother of God. By it was a plaque in Latin. Mr Eyton explained it was a memorial to a little girl, Florence Allcard, who had lived but 11 months and died 21 years ago. I felt sad for the rest of the day, especially for the mother who was still grieving after such a long time.

*Thursday 2nd July*. Horribly hot day. Dada says it reminds him of the Crimea. Nonetheless, at Mam's insistence we all went to the opening of the new chapel in Graham Street. I don't remember much, except the stifling heat, the interminable sermon and the smell and crush of people. Couldn't really see what the inside of the building looked like there were so many there.

*Friday 3rd July*. On my way back from work I bumped into Mr Eyton who was in bubbling form and obviously very delighted with the events of the previous day. He informed me that the practice of tipping the pew openers is to be forbidden and then with great ceremony lent me (he stressed lent) a copy of the *Church Times*, from which I quote. "Yesterday being the festival of the Visitation BVM, a mission chapel in Graham Street, Pimlico, a portion of the parish of St Paul's, Knightsbridge, far distant from the church in Wilton Place, was opened for service under the licence of the Bishop of London. The service at 11 o'clock was well attended by people from the neighbourhood and we were glad to notice a good sprinkling of poor women. Mr Eyton, the curate-in-charge, was the celebrant and an unconscionably long sermon was preached by Mr Knox Little, which considering the broiling weather was little better than cruelty. When will preachers learn that on such occasions—if there must be a sermon, the desirableness of which is by no means clear—a quarter of an hour is ample time to devote to it? The chapel, built with brick, from the designs of Mr RJ Withers, is in the early English style. A spacious nave is terminated in an apsidal-chancel and there are two aisles. The nave is very lofty and the interior of the roof is elaborately decorated with colour. Bold figures of Our Lady and St John on either side of the crucifix appear on the reredos, in front of which stands one of the most effective altars we have seen of late. It is formed of sweet cedar, and is richly ornamented with gold and colour. The chapel as a whole is remarkably effective, and has a solid and substantial look which is highly satisfactory. It is, in a word, an excellent specimen of an inexpensive church, the cost of the whole, not counting special gifts such as the reredos, altar, font, etc., being about £4,500, which considering that it will hold 550 worshippers, is a really moderate sum. The offertory at the early Celebration yesterday was £38.15s and at the 11 o'clock Celebration £200. We beg to congratulate Mr Liddell on the completion of a work in which he has taken much interest."

*Saturday 4th July.* Took an evening stroll along the Embankment eastwards and was very depressed by the vast Government Military Clothing Stores; the people working there must feel like so many million ants. Millbank prison is even gloomier, but at least its denizens are not there by choice. Dad says I'm a sentimental young fool.

*Sunday 5th July.* Returned the *Church Times* to Mr Eyton who told me that the St Mary's Parochial Excursion to Hatfield on the Bank Holiday will cost 2/-. I'm definitely going. Mr Eyton told me that William and Emily were seriously thinking about joining the party.

*Monday 6th July.* A statue of the immortal Bard has been erected in Leicester Square and, according to the newspaper, what was a deserted waste land has been turned into a blooming garden. All the surrounding houses and especially the Hôtel de l'Europe were festooned with coloured flags and bannerets.

*Saturday 11th July.* Eton has won the annual match against Harrow by five wickets. I was not there (joke!).

*Monday 3rd August.* The great excursion to Hatfield! We all went: Mam, Dada, Rose and Ada but not, obviously, Philip, who is in France, nor James who was on guard duty. I couldn't believe it, there were more than 500 of us on the special train. Dada was a bit annoyed at having to sign a pledge that he would not enter a public house or drink any intoxicating liquor until his return home. But he came nonetheless.

The moment we arrived at the Park the amusements began. Most of the men went off to the cricket ground, but I decided I would visit the house, to which we had graciously been invited by Lord Salisbury himself. This is not entirely true, because I was drifting to the cricket ground when I espied Emily—whom I had not seen on the train—mounting the steps of the house and I decided then and there to change my plan. I caught up with her in the hall, a magnificent and ancient room. She seemed surprised, but pleased to see me, having assumed that I had joined William at the cricket match. A lady, somebody said it was indeed the Marchioness, talked about the house, but such was the throng of people it was hard to discern what she was saying. We were allowed over almost all the house, upstairs and down; it was very rich and fine. I particularly liked the portraits of Queen Elizabeth and Mary Queen of Scots by Nicholas Hilliard. They did make me think that those French painters whose work I had seen in Paris, just a few months ago, had something to learn from the past. It was also very affecting seeing a hat, gloves and stockings that Queen Elizabeth had worn.

After that we joined the others in the grounds to watch the races. I was cajoled by Emily to take part in a sprint, though I hardly excelled myself. She herself, however, won her event, and it was a joy to watch her, albeit flying over the ground, like a filly.

The games continued and at the same time there was dancing to a first rate band. I did dance with Emily twice, but, never having been taught, I am not much good with my feet, so instead persuaded her to stroll around the gardens.

At four o'clock there was tea in a tent and a grand meal it was. Cold pies of all sorts: chicken and ham, steak and kidney and oyster, and salmagundi, followed by great bowls of strawberries and raspberries with cream. And to drink there was tea and lemonade. More dancing after this, Emily and I deciding to sit it out as we had eaten rather a lot. Mr Eyton then announced what he described as the crowning excitement of the day: the tug-of-war between the married ladies and the single. It was stubborn stuff and, at times, heated. The roars of the supporters were quite deafening. I was both embarrassed and proud that my own dear Mam had been coerced into joining the married ladies' team. Embarrassed, because it was hardly a lady-like affair, but proud, because time after time they worsted their opponents. Then there was prize giving and Emily was presented with a leather bound book of prayers for winning her event.

And then it was the end of the day. And what a day! I slept on the train on the way home, though I could dimly hear others singing. I don't think I have ever had such a tiring or such a happy day. I knew I would sleep like a baby and I did.

*Friday 14th August.* Our cousin, Mr Henry Nye of 1 Eaton Cottages came to sweep the chimneys and beat the carpets. He is a comical man, but I fear Dada looks down on him. I asked Mr Ketteringham if I might take his daughter out on a pleasure boat excursion and he has agreed. Hooray!

*Sunday 16th August.* Part of Dada's growing-up advice. Always avoid Temperance Hotels, strange as it may appear, he says they are neither clean nor economical.

*Thursday 20th August.* I read this in a magazine of Mam's and believe it worthy of recording: "The most reliable symptoms of fine weather are a gradually rising barometer, a grey morning sky, a red sunset, a light blue mid-day sky and dew at any time. A steadily falling barometer, a red sunrise, a pale yellow sky, low soft-looking dingy clouds, unusual distinctness of the landscape, much twinkling of the stars, and low flight of birds indicate rain. Sudden changes of the barometer, a bright yellow sunset with rosy tints in the east, rapidly driving scud and a deep blue sky foretell wind and stormy weather."

*Sunday 23rd August.* From the above I deemed I had chosen the right day for my boat excursion with Emily, for there had been a red sunset the night before and early in the morning it was grey and misty. After eight o'clock Holy Communion at St Mary's we took the Inner Circle line from Sloane Square to Paddington and from there walked up to the Canal Bridge at Bishops Road to embark on Mr G Brooks' pleasure boat. The fare to Greenford Green and back was 1/4d, which I thought very reasonable.

The boat was nearly full, but having arrived early we managed to get seats on the side. Emily was wearing a flowery pink and green frock with a little straw sun hat and I felt proud to be her companion. We chugged along the waterway past green fields and woodlands, stopping first at the Junction Arms at Willesden, then on to Alperton and Horsenden Hill and ending up at Greenford Green near Harrow, where the famous public school is. Public that is only if you can afford the £25.0.0. a year fees.

We had some time before our return trip, so we sat on the grass and ate the picnic Mam had provided for us. She had said the refreshments offered by the boat company would be dear and meagre. She had given us chicken wings and hard boiled eggs and ham sandwiches and cherries and a bottle of elderflower wine. I happen to think that this must have been not without alcohol because I began to feel somewhat inspired and found myself holding Emily's hand. "Emily, your hand is very small and soft." "Is it?" "Well, I mean compared to mine." "That I cannot deny."

She smiled up at me. I felt as if the sun had rushed through my whole body. "Emily, may I ask you a question?" "If it's as to more to eat, I've had more than ample." "No, I was just wondering. When you get married, where do you think it will be?" "Oh, I suppose at St Mary's, by Mr Eyton. Why do you ask?"

And then she squeezed my hand.

Notes
1. Coleshill Street is now Eaton Terrace.
2. Master Nye is out by one day. The Marquess was raised to a Dukedom on the 27th February 1874.
3. Now Graham Terrace.
4. Now St Mary's Presbytery, 30 Bourne Street. The engraved glass window of the old pub is now part of the ground floor office. Explorers of the undercroft can see where the beer barrels once rolled into the cellar.
5. The expression lives on in a pub of that name in Falcon Road, Battersea.
6. A 125 years later the gasometers still function on the south side of Chelsea Bridge, while Price's Candles continue to trade from their works in York Road.
7. A regional term for a gypsy, now rarely encountered.
8. Since the early 1970s an office block facing Victoria Station on Buckingham Palace Road.
9. Westbourne Street is now Bourne Street.
10. Master Nye is presumably thinking of the dish *La Poule au Pot*, originally associated with Henri IV. There is now a restaurant of that name on the corner of Ebury Street, though it did not, of course, exist at the time of the diary.
11. Master Nye has his genders confused here. B(erthe) Morisot was, of course, a woman.

# Like no other parish

## *Fr Whitby appoints a new curate ~ Fr David Powell*

I ARRIVED at the presbytery for an interview in the spring of 1936. Fr Whitby took me round. I shall refer to him as HW, which is how he signed notes. Nobody, not even his closest friends, so far as I know, called him 'Humphrey'. His greatest friend and he called each other Mr Whitby and Mr Child. For some reason he pretended to dislike 'Father' preferring 'Mr', but the parish started calling him 'Sir' which he didn't like either. I never heard anyone trying 'Vicar' on him. He soon reverted to 'Father', which we all called him whether in his presence or not. He told me once that the parish boys called him (in his absence) Charlie, but I doubt if this was true. I pronounce my name with the first syllable rhyming with 'roe' and learnt with embarrassment that the boys referred to me as 'Fr Chamberwell'. I regret that the recherché counter-reformation atmosphere of St Mary's could only produce this deplorable pun.

HW told me a bit about the parish. He said that there were those young clergymen (he seldom said 'priest'—and indeed never 'clergy' when he meant 'clergymen') who would give their eyes to be on St Mary's staff and who thought that it consisted of "strolling up and down the predella" and (but not presumably at that time) sipping sherry, but that in fact it was no bed of roses. This proved to be so.

The staff normally consisted of a senior curate together with a junior. The latter never seemed to last long. This was hardly so, however, for Peter Clear, who got his title at St Mary's in 1936 and only left in 1939 to be a naval chaplain. I came in at the end of the reign of many years of Philip Audley Brown (known as PAB). He was a model priest, a dictator, frightening till you knew his kind heart; a perfectionist. He seldom preached, for he was not good at it and I think he had some private means. He lived in one of the flats on the second floor, disliked central heating and had a coal fire which the houseboy had to look after. He was 'good with lads' in the best sense of that phrase, and ran the Scouts. The parish boys of that age and a few of the choir (who were not 'parish') were organized through Scouts and through a club which was in the basement. They were privileged and allowed to use the basement bathroom. He also ran the Senior Catechism and gave the homily while HW gave the instruction.

The boys were all in the Ward of St Martin in the Confraternity of Our Most Holy Redeemer, which was the medium by which the whole congregation was run, with wards for both sexes and all age groups—St John the Evangelist for adult men, St Anne for older women, St Michael for older boys, St Martin for younger, St Agnes for girls. Each ward wore its livery on the occasions of processions and watches before the Holy Sacrament. These were on Maundy Thursday, during Exposition from the morning of the Saturday after Corpus Christi till the procession of the Host on the Sunday evening; the Mary procession (on some May Sunday evening); the St George's procession (with emphasis on Scouts) in his octave; the Feast of Title procession on the evening of the Sunday after July 2nd; and the Visitation.

The Scout summer camp was in a village near the Norfolk coast and the camp's elaborate arrangements had to be seen to be believed. There was little scouting as such in PAB's time, nor did the boys have to do many chores so far as I could see, when I stayed at the camp the summer before I went to St Mary's. The boys were given a jolly good holiday. There was perfect discipline. Cooking was done by a male volunteer. There were complete sets of vestments for the daily mass which all attended. I was there for Assumption eve when PAB was in the confessional calling the next penitent's name (like a GP in an NHS surgery). I don't think anyone thought of not complying. One morning they would go to Walsingham and sing and serve a mass in the Shrine.

At St Mary's the 7am daily mass was served by boys, the 8am by men. Spikes and others from outside were discouraged! The 10am Sunday mass was also served by boys. It was sung with incense and an address but with no communions save that of the celebrant. The hymns were usually the same and the ordinary was sung to a mixture

of Merbeck and *Missa de Angelis*. The High Mass at 11am was probably largely as it is now. Any visiting preacher sat on a special chair
on the Gospel side under the gallery and delivered the sermon after
the Blessing. If there was no visiting preacher, then there was a hymn
after the Blessing and during it people escaped from the sermon!
But there was no escaping from a visiting preacher for there was no
hymn. HW would occasionally invite preachers who were not
accustomed to the ways of St Mary's (they were sometimes members
of his club, the United Universities). They were nervous of the
ceremonial yet expected to be involved in it. They often arrived
carrying a bag of robes, which they were discouraged from wearing.
One of the sisters would see they put on a cotta specially designed
for St Mary's clergymen. This sort of 'special' preacher did not like it
when he found after all he was completely ignored in the ceremonial. When sermon time came he was ushered into the pulpit (then
on the other side and very modest) by the verger. The ceremonial
itself was never fussy nor did the servers try to look pious. There was
attached to the west gallery a clock [since stolen] which chimed the
quarter hours. The sacristy bell had to be rung immediately after the
chime and of course the procession had to come in—a great trial for
me as priest sacristan.

The 12.15 mass with music was served by senior men and all
Low Masses were served in lay dress. The congregation remained
silent throughout except in a dialogue mass which took place at
8am, I think, on the third Sunday of the month. This was also the
day the boys and girls of the parish kept the Confraternity rule
of Communion once a month. The 12.15 mass (also known as the
"Hangover Mass") on Sundays (not held from after Goodwood till
Michaelmas) was drowned by music, sometimes organ only, sometimes with a vocalist or violinist. HW once got a fit of Protestantism
and ordered silence for the Gospel and Elevations. This service was
meant for actors, actresses and others who had had a night out. You
could also kick into it boys who had not yet fulfilled their obligation
before they were allowed into the club.

In the summer of 1939 HW was immersed in his Cranmerian

studies in his room at the top of the presbytery. Peter Clear and I had in our individual ways kept organizations going. While he looked after the elder boys, I was inflicted with Cubs and the Senior Catechism. Guiding and Brownies were the responsibility of Misses Quarmby and Redman. They also ran an innovation—a mixed social club. Miss Redman still keeps up with some of them. That year organizations were so full and flourishing that the July procession had to go out of doors as it would have snarled up inside the church.

The week before September 3rd everything flopped like a collapsing tent. There was a mass exodus of children into the country and very few people of any age were left. Peter very soon departed to become a Naval Chaplain. There seemed nothing to do save paste black paper over windows.

The two basement clubrooms became shelters for HW, Leonard Gabb (the bachelor churchwarden who occupied one of the second-floor flats), the domestic staff, and guests, who were frequent. Dom Gregory Dix was a friend of HW (though differing in views on Cranmer and liturgy). The former, however, refused to descend to the basement but braved air attack in a top floor guest room. On the other hand Maurice Child would prefer to sleep on a camp bed below clad in nothing but a silk dressing gown. This was obviously how he would like to appear either before the divine judge or to the vulgar gaze if bombed out.

There was also an extremely high priest whom we shall refer to as Fr X. His preference was for silk cassock and biretta. What he wore under the cassock I know not, but beneath the hat was a double first. He had been bombed out of a church on the south coast and was teaching in a suburban prep. school. HW was kind to him mainly because he liked to pick his brains over translations for the new Anglican Missal (which like all HW's literary efforts never got published). They would confer at length in HW's room on how to iron out the mixed metaphors in the Sacred Heart preface. I dropped a clanger once at breakfast on the Feast of the Seven Sorrows. X was present and I poured scorn on the very poor translation of the Stabat Mater in the English Missal (which against all Whitbeian principles

I had to use as there was only one tattered Anglican Missal at St Mary's except a very carefully preserved copy for HW's use only). HW afterwards told me that it was X who had perpetrated the translation I so much despised. I had indeed noticed a painful silence.

I liked to tease X. He had some sense of humour but none relating to either breviary or missal, the Latin editions of which he kissed before and after use. On the feast of SS Cosmas and Damian, again over breakfast, I told him I had a problem. On the commemoration of a saint mentioned in the canon of the Mass you were supposed to give a slight bow at the mention of his name. But this bow in the case of a saint was only to be made in the direction of the missal and not towards the altar cross. What then was one to do on the Feast of Cosmas and Damian—nod to the book at Cosmas, turn the head to the centre and then nod to the book at Damian, or make one turn to the book end nod twice and then turn the head to the centre (or for that matter—and I have only just thought of this—I wish I had thought of it then—make only one nod for the mention of the two saints)? This drivel produced a deep and serious silence on the part of X, who was nonplussed and said he had never thought of that.

On another occasion he was celebrating an 11 o'clock mass on Sunday at St Mary's, which at this point in the war was reduced to Low Mass with hymns. They even had to rely on the writer as organist. X raced through the mass and rushed to Westminster Cathedral in order to attend the Low Mass with hymns there. Those were the days. But Fr X was a kindly and probably misunderstood man.

HW was not the sort of man who liked putting out fires caused by enemy action but he realised his duty and was a member of my fire watching team. Two fire bombs fell on the church, but they were both duds. One was on the choir room roof and the other penetrated the nave and fell on the floor. In conversation I once said to HW "If the church is hit" and he quickly shut me up with "St Mary's will never be hit". He was a man of deep prayer and I believe he had a deal with our Lady about this. After all, did she not enfold the church in her arms on the cover of the *Quarterly*? He attended only one fire watching practice which took place in the basement bathroom with the local air raid warden, a stirrup pump and the writer. HW was in his steel helmet, carrying gasmask and standing with his back to the lift and attending to the instructions. However, after a short time there was a quiet clicking noise. HW was bored and had ascended to his rooms.

There he endlessly dictated through a machine his work on Cranmer, the prayer books of 1549, 1552 and the rest. He sought to show that the prayer book of 1662 was a catholic document. If this were not so, he could not have remained in the Church of England. The abortive books of 1927 and 1928 had upset him so much that he took a sabbatical and went to South America, *en voyage* to meditate and pray about these matters. He returned having decided against Rome, but the catholicity of the Prayer Book was desperately important to him. He was frantically opposed to that of 1928. The fact that there are so many copies of the Book of Common Prayer in St Mary's is because he bought hundreds during this crisis. If St Mary's were to opt out of the Church of England, the building would have to stay in the established church, but there was Carmel Hall, which was not diocesan property but belonged to St Mary's Trust. And the BCP might go out of print! HW was a quiet man, but any remark concerning this book or that of 1928 with which he did not agree would lead to a face as red as a turkey cock and an angry and impassioned outburst. The only other times I saw this happen were when I lost my master key to church and presbytery, and when three o'clock lunch on Good Friday was late in coming up in the dumb waiter.

When I was interviewed for the job HW told me two things: not to do physical exercises in my bedroom nude without curtains drawn across the windows (lest pupils at the school opposite be scandalized—this apparently had occurred); and never to use the Roman canon. HW was convinced that the 1662 book contained a valid Eucharistic rite, but that the 1552 preface said that the former book (1549) was a "very godly order." All depended on the meaning

---

of 'order.' Thus, basically 1662 was used but with 1549 additions and order of rite. The story went that the silent canon came into use in the old Lord Halifax's time as churchwarden. He was strict in his views on audibility but at the same time was exceedingly deaf. Thus honour was satisfied. The result of course was that a stranger attending St Mary's thought he was in a very high church indeed. However, he would not think it Roman, for Latin was scarcely heard (except in the refrain of "Though the Streets of Heaven", a Marian processional hymn, Appendix I). Polyphony was sung in English.

A curate's life at St Mary's in the pre-war 1930s was different from that of other parishes in that you had your self-contained flat. HW used to say you could die in your bed and no-one would know for days. A loud electric bell like a burglar alarm would sound in the bedroom at any hour you asked. It was operated from the housekeeper's bedroom. I recollect, however, one difficult couple (housekeeper and husband) who could not be persuaded to perform this service.

Sunday worship started at 7am with Low Mass at the high altar. There would be some 20 in church. About three-quarters of the congregation communicated in one kind. I never understood how this came about. HW obviously did not really like communion in one kind, otherwise he would not have directed that children be instructed to communicate in both, which is what they all did. A priest offering the chalice had to be wary, for strangers who devoutly bowed the head at Communion would expect the chalice, whereas at St Mary's to the *cognoscenti* to bow was the sign you did not wish it. Why you could not simply retire from the rail I did not know. To my knowledge this misunderstanding led to at least two devout Catholics attending St Mary's for the first time (on the recommendation of my father, who was a priest) becoming very embarrassed at being passed by and left high and dry. They never entered the church again. They were St Mary's loss and the gain respectively of St Stephen's, Gloucester Road, and St Saviour's, Walton Street.

At Low Mass (normally at the high altar with of course the Holy Sacrament reserved) the first act upon the priest's entry was the server ringing a bell for communicants to approach the altar. This was for workers who had no time to attend mass. Low Mass thus was like this: Communion (Roman use but with Prayer Book Confession and Absolution); Preparation (aloud not muttered); Collect for Purity whispered; altar kissed as you said the end of the prayer; Introit; Kyrie in Greek; possibly Gloria; Collect(s) (Missal rules were observed but Prayer Book forms took precedence); Epistle and Gradual etc; "cleanse my heart"; Gospel ("the continuation of the Holy Gospel" being the introduction); (Creed); Offertory Sentence from the Missal; Offertory prayers; the Secret Prayer was the prayer for the church militant but—wait for it—instead of "Pray, brethren" we twisted round and said "Let us pray" and the rest of the words (for the whole state" etc) whispered, the answer being "the Lord receive etc"; Sursum Corda etc with Benedictus; then you recited the Prayer of Consecration making the manual acts as best you might and so on with 'silent' consecration; Prayer of Oblation 'silently' with manual acts (HW told me to put in the Anamnesis); Lord's Prayer with 1549 introduction, Peace, Fraction; after the 'silent' prayer for unity you said the Prayer of Humble Access 'silently' (Fr Langton started saying it in the medium voice); then came the Roman Communion devotions but with Prayer Book Confession and Absolution; Ablutions of course—whether you had them here or at the end was a criterion of mediocrity or highness— 'TARP' meant "taking the ablutions at the right place." A popular clerihew went: "St Polycarp/Refused to tarp/St John his friend/Always took 'em at the end"); Post-Communion Sentence followed by the thanksgiving prayer from BCP adding other prayers as required; blessing and "ite, missa est" (yes, we said this in Latin), or whatever was appropriate; Last Gospel (the young will need this explained—St John's prologue said aloud); Leo XIII's prayers after mass (this was the only part of the service the congregation joined in—the priest usually spoke louder and the people responded heartily). I have omitted to say that the proper "The Lord be with yous" were inserted. This was a lovely service both for celebrant and people. It is a pity it was ever altered.

A rubric at the end of service timetables said that a priest could be seen between the 7am and 8am masses. This sounded rather like a haunting but meant that you went into the confessional, specially on Sundays. This was a real help to shy sinners and those who could not last the Saturday night without a fall. HW always insisted the confessional be free, that is to say with no claims to "my penitents". He particularly objected to clergymen referring to "one of my penitents".

Sick communions were weekly. You usually took these at 7.30 wearing cloak and round beaver hat (not omitting buckled shoes) preceded by a sister ringing a bell. There were two sick, however, who were communicated by me conveyed in an ancient Rolls. The chauffeur placed a fur rug round your knees and then the great vehicle slowly ground its way to an address in Eaton Square, where a footman let you in, and where inside the husband of the patient greeted the sacrament with a lighted candle and conducted you upstairs in a lift. The chariot then took you to Hans Crescent where a rich and dear friend (she was Prices' candles) received the sacrament. Breakfast was, I recollect, at half past eight but you could still get it at nine.

Once a week, I believe, I taught a class at St Barnabas' school. This was good, as we had not a few of our children there, and it helped to bring the two parishes together.

Before the war there was no other service during the week except on Saturday evenings, when there were said Evensong and Matins followed by simple Benediction. During the war we said daily Evensong followed by simple Adoration (as I should have called it). 'Adoration' was HW''s name for 'devotions'. All was done as at Benediction except that the Host was held up before the people without making the sign of the cross.

The Parish Mass was a jolly affair, and it was served by younger boys, who had to attend mass if they wished to use the club. Quite right too. At High Mass the choir consisted of paid men, very highly qualified (we pinched the best counter-tenor in London from Our Lady of Victories, Kensington—our victory this time) and boys mainly from George Underwood's school at St Matthias, Earl's Court. Their tone was fairly rough, not 'cathedral'. The polyphony invariably sung satisfied my artistic tastes but hearing the present choir I realise that standards have gone up market. But the music was lovely, though Underwood was not much of an organist although the choir were devoted to him. The 12.15 mass was never taken by the three of us but usually by the saintly Fr Bignold SSJE, from St Edward's House. He was stone deaf and so the music at this mass would not have disturbed him. For a time after HW's retirement he would come up for the weekend using one of the guest rooms and his private masseur would attend him on Sunday morning.

A feature of St Mary's was the Joyous Pageant of the Nativity. Some time in the twenties a man called Charles Claye asked HW if he could produce his pageant in Carmel Hall. It had been conceived and born in Derby, where Claye came from. HW somewhat reluctantly gave permission but was soon converted and by the time I arrived the Pageant was part of the scene, though it was never regarded as stemming from St Mary's. The cast came from all over the place. I am not sure if the adult members of the cast had to be Anglican communicants, but our Lady had to be a virgin. The only professional ever to take part was someone who played St Joseph. I felt honoured to be asked to play this part in 1939, but of course that year the Pageant was never performed. One year I understudied one of the Kings and on one occasion I played Simeon, so that HW, who always played this, could see the scene from the front. It was an amateur show professionally produced. Charles Claye was a dwarf and a cripple who swung along on crutches. He had a high piping voice. He was deeply religious and a very sensitive artist.

The Pageant was partly mime, partly movement with no speaking, except that our Lady uttered the first words of the Magnificat. The scenes were modelled on and in some cases were exact copies of *quatrocento* and later masters. Music arranged and composed by Anthony Bernard made the whole an inspiration. There was nothing really like it anywhere else. It was performed about every other year and in the Chelsea Palace Theatre. There were several performances during Advent but never after Christmas. Some people would attend all performances. There was much competition for children to take parts of cherubs and innocents. The Pageant was revived by Fr Langton but ceased at Claye's death. I saw the script once in, of all places, the YMCA in Algiers during the war, but I imagine the choreography and decor were in Claye's brain and died with him. The Pageant was partly a product of the Catholic Movement in the '20s and '30s and perhaps could not be repeated now. Claye was a meek man except at rehearsals. He was very angry if you were late whoever you were. He became a great friend of HW. I never knew where he lived. I think he was a man of some means. For a period during the war he lived at the presbytery occupying the top guest room that gives on to Bourne Street. He was delightful at meals and he spent much time praying before the Holy Sacrament.

I think we thought we were the elite of Anglican Holy Week worshippers and perhaps we were. Things were done as can be found in an old Anglican Missal. I remember that on the first Palm Sunday that I was there HW, who always celebrated the High Mass on that day, left out a whole section of the rite and no one noticed. This was because his eyes were very weak and he missed his place in the book. The MC on that day was not very experienced and failed to correct him. I was hovering about somewhere and was far too scared to run in. On Palm Sunday evening Stations were made instead of a sermon and O *Saviour of the world* (Goss) was sung as a recessional— an unusual piece of music for the choir, who went to town at Tenebrae (ie matins of Thursday, Friday and Saturday in Holy Week sung at 8pm the night before). There was a hearse placed in the sanctuary although this was not a limousine but a triangular candle stand with unbleached candles (one, I think, for each verse of the Benedictus) with a bleached candle at the top. This was moved and hidden at the end of the benedictus and brought back again, to symbolize the death and resurrection. But the highlight was the singing of the responds between the lessons. The composers of these services were varied from the 16th century onwards. One set was Victorian by, I believe, an uncle of mine named Cyril Miller, who was priest-organist at St Cuthbert's, Philbeach Gardens. (The sort of joke one made in those days was to call it St Filbert's, Cuthbeach Gardens.) This music was ravishing and congregations were large. There was also a devotion known as "Bona Mors", which was a kind of litany sung at adoration on the Monday of Holy Week. High Mass of Maundy Thursday was at 6.30pm and a watch was kept until the Good Friday morning (not afternoon) liturgy. Women were not allowed to watch after 10pm. There were official watchers, male and female, supplied by ward members of the Confraternity, two each. The women wore veils, the men a sash.

On Good Friday at about 4pm the relic of the True Cross was exposed and venerated at the altar of the Seven Sorrows. This was never performed by HW who never attended. However, he (and never, so far as I recollect, any of the staff) conducted the Stations of the Cross backwards (not walking backwards but starting at XIV and ending at I) to be with our Lady as she recalled the footsteps of the Passion. The Holy Saturday rites were of course in the morning, at 10am lasting till about 12.30. There was a full church for this. HW never came in at the start but hovered about somewhere producing the holy oils at the appropriate moment at the font. One year the rite was photographed by the press from the gallery and written up in a popular Sunday paper. HW only gave leave for this on condition I was not told beforehand. As I was the officiant this was sensible and kind of him. There was a picture of the young priest smilingly refusing a cigarette outside the vestry door after this 'marathon' rite. It took time to live all this down.

Benediction was introduced through HW's friend Langton, although HW was the first to conduct the service at St Mary's. Solemn Benediction was the climax of exposition within the octave of Corpus Christi from the Saturday morning until Sunday evening. We had then (and I suppose you have now) a magnificent baroque monstrance, but I imagine its lunette now fits a large Host. HW had had it fitted for a people's Host, in order, one assumes, to emphasize that consecration was for communion of the faithful and not solely for adoration. Of course this argument would not apply these days, as breaking a large Host for communion of the people is common, but it certainly was not then.

You still have the throne for the monstrance behind the high altar. Special steps were placed there in my time to reach it. If one was a minister in Solemn Adoration it was an embarrassment holding this heavy monstrance and coping with the skirts of one's cassock and alb. Adding to these difficulties was the local usage of holding the Blessed Sacrament before the people using ciborium not monstrance (this was to avoid offending the Bishop). Thus the minister or assistant priest had to take a small Host from the ciborium, place it in the lunette and fix the latter in the monstrance. Then later he had to bring the monstrance down, open it, place the small Host in the ciborium again. This all took time and one visiting preacher told me afterwards that he thought I might have got into some difficulty and nearly walked up to see what he could do to help. On one of these occasions we had the honour of a visit from gentlemen of the Kensit persuasion. One of them wrote us up in their magazine and it made good reading. It was correct reporting, though words such as "host," "monstrance" or "altar" were printed with quotation marks. And so it was that in the course of the proceedings a young "priest" took the "monstrance" and perched (sic) it on a high ledge above. I felt proud as I was that young priest, that percher.

Though many might not have thought it, HW was keenly interested in Biblical (as well as sacramental) exposition. Dr Campbell Morgan held weekly expositions at Westminster Chapel and at one period HW attended them and I went with him once. He decided to run weekly Bible services on Wednesday evenings before the war. He often said that he could always rely on 60 of the faithful to turn up at anything he laid on, and this proved so. He took great trouble with preparation and ran an excellent course on the Revelation of St John. His treatment of course was conservative. He used copious notes and had a specially high pulpit lectern constructed for focusing his very poor eyes. However, there was another occasion on which he did not summon his faithful although many turned up. This was just after Munich in 1938. Fr Clear and I attended a ruridecanal meeting (HW only once attended to my knowledge) and we came back full of enthusiasm for some sort of thanksgiving campaign for what we nearly all thought was escape from the prospect of war. So we asked HW if we could organize a service and circularise the parish, and he consented, albeit rather coolly. He didn't think anyone would come. Peter got an attractive handbill printed and arranged for the Scouts to deliver it at every house in the parish (there were more then). I took the simple service from the pulpit. It consisted of hymns, prayers and an address and the church was absolutely packed. We had caught people on the wave of a great feeling of relief. Sadly, this effort did not mean that a single extra soul came to church. Incidentally, we found that during the war and in particular during the blitz, fear of loss of property, injury or death seemed not to drive folk to their knees, at any rate not in church.

Another aspect of HW's ministry, which might have surprised people, was his desire to achieve more understanding between Evangelicals and folk of our ilk. He made friends with those at Holy Trinity, Brompton (then an extreme Evangelical centre) and arranged periodic meetings, although I don't think they got anywhere. HW used to say that they showed absolutely no interest in the Epistle to the Hebrews. One meeting was at the presbytery. I was never asked to the meetings but on this occasion we all had a stand up lunch in the dining room. The Evangelical leader and Vicar of Holy Trinity, Brian Green, asked HW who that nice young man was (meaning me). Believe me, I was thrilled!

I do not know of any existing former member of St Mary's staff who remains unmarried save one, but I suppose we were considered in a vague way to be celibate. The subject was rarely mentioned. HW would sometimes make snide (a word not then in use) remarks against clergy wives, but he must have been careful as he knew I was a son of the manse. There were stories (among many such going round about St Mary's) that no married clergyman was ever allowed either to celebrate or to preach. But this was untrue. Actually, the clergymen he would not have were those he considered to have blotted their copybook with modernistic views. It would be unfair to mention names, but I can think of one priest with whom he used to be very friendly and who was thus barred but received back as it were, into communion later, the Reverend Dudley Symon, headmaster of Woodbridge, was married, a well known preacher and a favourite in St Mary's pulpit. As for celebrating, Minor Canon Reece (with a wife and many children) used regularly to say a weekday mass during the war, as did the lovable Canon Demant, likewise married, who rode a bicycle from St Paul's through the city. And HW used to say that training in our theological colleges was not geared to celibacy. Celibate, however, he was. Although he had many women friends, he was very shy and was never seen shaking hands after a service. At the time of the construction of the north aisle a covered passage along the outside wall from the crypt stairs to the sacristy was mooted and was to be called 'the path that no fowl knoweth'. HW's normal way of entering the church was out of the front door (he invariably used the lift), along Graham Terrace and to what I irreverently call the stage door.

I never heard HW remark upon Walsingham. He was a Founder Guardian yet never erected a shrine in church. But he would attend most regularly the guardian meetings. He travelled in his Rover chauffeured by his secretary, Mr Williamson, accompanied by Sir Eric Maclagan, Director of the Victoria and Albert Museum and a most devout churchman and fellow guardian, and they put up at a good hotel in Norwich. HW's piety was deep but he was not the kind to be seen putting up candles or for that matter praying before the Sacrament. He usually celebrated on weekdays at 7am. Then the verger would bring him a cup of tea from the presbytery afterwards and HW would take sips whilst meditating standing on one leg and leaning against the vesting table in the inner sacristy. Surprisingly, he was not a punctual person and would arrive in the sacristy for mass about two minutes to the hour, sometimes later. I disappeared in 1942 to be a naval chaplain and then to work in UNCA. St Mary's was kind enough to keep my name on the staff list till I suggested to Canon Nicholson it be deleted. But I have ever since felt St Mary's blood flowing in my veins.

# The Home of the Faith

*Spoken Word and Broken Word ~ John Greenhalgh*

## The Historical Background

WHEN ST MARY'S was dedicated in 1874, the Oxford Movement was 40 years old. Keble's famous Assize Sermon, WG Ward's *The Ideal of a Christian Church*, the *Tracts for the Times*, Newman's secession (1845)—all these were things of the past by 1874. So, indeed, were the infamous riots which had occurred in 1850–1 in St Barnabas and which forced the resignation of Mr Bennett, the vicar of St Paul's, Knightsbridge, with its chapelry of St Barnabas.[1] Against all the theoretical odds, the vast majority of Tractarians were happy to remain in the Church of their birth, continuing to show conspicuous loyalty to their Anglican inheritance. They were still able to accept the Church of England as both the true historic Catholic Church of this land[2] and a Divine institution,[3] that is part of the mystical body of Christ to which clergy and laity belong equally.

As St Mary's opened its doors for the first time, the Oxford Movement was entering a new and crucial phase of its growth and development. Through the Public Worship Regulation Act and the Church Association, opponents of the movement were attempting to eradicate all forms of ritualism.[4] At the same time the "Six Points" initiative, which sought to restore the Eastward Position, Eucharistic Vestments, the Mixed Chalice, Altar Candles, Unleavened Bread and Incense (and similar ceremonial) in the celebration of the Holy Communion, was given wider publicity by the English Church Union. The ebb and flow of the struggle has been well documented. Two events more than anything else finally discredited the Protestant opposition. The first was the imprisonment, between 1877 and 1882, for ritualistic offences, of four priests (Arthur Tooth, Thomas Pelham Dale, Richard William Erraght and Sidney Faithorn Green). The second was the Lincoln Judgement of 1890 which upheld Bishop King in his introduction of the singing of the Agnus Dei and the making of the sign of the Cross in blessing and absolving during public worship.

Time passed. The word 'Tractarian' and the expression 'Oxford Movement' were used less frequently to describe what was happening to an increasing extent in the Church of England, namely an emphasis on the dogmatic and sacramental content of Christian belief and practice. More popular were the terms High Church and Anglo-Catholic.[5] St Mary's was in the vanguard of the High Church/Anglo-Catholic tradition from its very beginnings and has remained there ever since. The attitude towards liturgy at St Mary's was determined by what was believed about the nature of the Church. Liturgy demonstrated what was believed about the Faith and about the Worship of God. A 'High' interpretation of 'Church' produced in St Mary's a supernatural view of the liturgy.

What was happening in the Catholic wing of the Church of England was thus reflected in the parish of St Mary's, Bourne Street, which became a leader in many things which this volume deals with in detail, including liturgy. This Tractarian/High Church/Anglo-Catholic tradition is the historical background against which the achievements of the past 125 years must be set. It offers an answer to the questions: "Why did people come to St Mary's? Why do people continue to come to St Mary's?"

## The Individual Response

Despite rejecting the extreme anti-intellectualism of the belief that Holy Writ was the sole, absolute, verbally inerrant repository of divinely revealed truth, no one brought up in mainstream Anglicanism ever forgets the fact that the Word of God in Scripture, is central to Christianity. The Sixth Article of Religion makes it very clear: "Holy Scripture containeth all things necessary to salvation." At the same time, a Protestant upbringing frequently means that the person (through association) becomes aware that, while the Bible is central to living out a Christian vocation, if one is bereft of the sacraments, something of great significance and importance is missing. Of course, it's easy to say: "We read a lot about Paul preaching the Word, but not very much about him saying Mass!" But it's more complicated than this.[6] It concerns that 'salvation' referred to in Article VI, and which is a continuing process. We have been saved (conversion and baptism), we are being saved (a sacramental activity) and we shall be saved (judgement).

The importance given to these "effectual signs of grace", signs outward and physical but with an inward spiritual meaning, is what has and does attract people to St Mary's, as to all churches in the Anglican Catholic tradition. It is difficult to remember what normative Anglican practice in worship was like even as little as 50 years ago. Nor do I refer to extreme Evangelical religion but to the 'Broad' church. It was usual for parishes to have, as their weekly fare, Sung Matins and Evensong on a Sunday, augmented by an eight o'clock Holy Communion and (once a month) a Choral Communion after Matins for which the church would empty. A further service of Holy Communion might take place during the week for the Mothers' Union. And that was it! There was a hunger for more and it was out of that hunger that St Mary's came to serve many more people than those who lived within the parish boundaries.[7]

And yet, St Mary's pastoral priority has always been towards those living nearby, people for whom the practice of the Catholic Faith has been the only Christianity they have encountered. It has done this from the beginning, although this side of its ministry has reached progressively fewer people as time has passed. In 1999 St Mary's is a very small parish indeed numerically (under a half of what it was in 1874 and with a high proportion of these parishioners 'non-resident' at weekends). The really destructive thing was to pull down the heart of the parish in the 1950s to make way for the St Michael's School.[8] Finally, after the Clean Air Act in the 1960s and the end of London smogs, St Mary's parish became a more attractive place in which to live. The negative side to this has been that the properties, rebuilt, have simply been treated as an investment by absentee owners.

Given these changes, it is remarkable how much St Mary's has managed to continue as a parish church as well as a church which attracts an eclectic congregation to services not on offer in the same way elsewhere. It is local residents which enable us to have Mass twice a day during the week and Morning and Evening Prayer said publicly in church every day. A majority of these people may not live in the geographical parish, but they do live within a radius of a walk of 10 to 15 minutes, a perfectly normal and acceptable distance for a suburban church congregation. Moreover, a survey completed for one of the Sundays in September 1998 showed that, of the 125 communicants that day, while only 20 lived in the parish proper, another 30 actually walked (or cycled) to church. An extraordinary non-eclectic 40 per cent!

It is nevertheless true that, in the Church at large, St Mary's distinguished reputation has been based on the fact that (as well as being a parish church in the proper sense of serving the locality) it is also a 'shrine' church attracting people from far afield. It is hard to believe that this congregation (present chiefly at Sunday High Mass) did not, until the mid-1960s, receive communion during the mass. It was an ancient Anglo-Catholic custom to go to an early Low Mass for private devotion and the reception of the sacrament and to the (later) High Mass for 'worship'. That has now all gone, but what has remained is the firm teaching on sacramental worship, the relevance of daily mass, and extra-liturgical devotions such as Benediction of the Blessed Sacrament which have characterised all those parishes which stood up for the principles of the Oxford Movement.[9]

## The Theological Perspective

St Mary's has always managed to balance successfully those twin ingredients of true religion: Word and Sacrament. We inherit, theologically, the concepts of Word and Sacrament from Old Testament Judaism.[10] In the Old Testament they are represented by the mediation of two priests from the House of Levi, Moses and Aaron. The Word[11] of God is given to Man, exceptionally through Moses on Mount Sinai. In subordinate status is Aaron, the liturgical, cultic priest who bears witness, with oblation and sacrifice, to the actual revelation which came through Moses. Cultic worship in Judaism remains secondary to the veneration given to God's Word, and this remains so in Christianity, too, in spite of suspect medieval practices which still plague the Church.

Christians, like the Jews, have always had to face the problem of the relationship between the two priestly functions of the mediation of the Word of God and mediation through sacrificial witness. To many Anglicans, over the years from the beginnings of the Oxford Movement to the present day, it seemed that much of the worship in the Church of England had swung out of focus in the direction of Biblical idolatry. Equally, these Anglicans looked (from 1829 onwards) at the Roman Catholic Church to see the dangers of Levitical priesthood gone wild with notions of priestly 'power' over the sacraments and a debased form of Apostolic Succession ruling the day. Anglo-Catholicism produced a balanced theology and worship whose appeal has been lasting and which has been and still is a mark of St Mary's own life and witness. But it is still open to error.[12]

In the Old Testament the whole of liturgy was regarded as something initiated by God. It was God himself who provided the Sacrifice and the whole action is described as a divinely inspired response to God's Word.[13] The liturgical priest witnesses to the once-and-for-all events in Israel's history when God intervened, in the Exodus and at Sinai. There were, from the start, conflicts between the prophets and priests because the priestly activity in sacrificial witness tried to make itself independent of the priestly mediation of the Word of God. Consider the revolt of Aaron and Miriam against Moses: "Has God spoken only to Moses?" The answer was in the affirmative and Miriam was punished by becoming a leper and the 'shekinah' or Glory of God left the Tabernacle of Aaron. Consider the prophet Amos, whose preaching of the Word of God is as frightening as the Moses and Aaron conflict: "I hate, I despise your feasts, and I take no delight in your solemn assemblies. Even though you offer me your burnt offerings and cereal offerings, I will not accept them... But let justice roll down like waters, and righteousness like an ever-flowing stream."[14]

At this point in Israel's history, Isaiah enters and puts before Israel the vision of the Suffering Servant. As a lamb led to the slaughter the Servant embodies in flesh and blood the Covenant with Israel made by God. Isaiah is talking about the redemption of Israel through a sacrificial action of God himself. It points to the messianic redemption through that union of God and Man which is the proclamation of the Christian Gospel. But, in terms of historical development, we are not yet at the historical point of Incarnation. After the Exile it all went wrong again with the 'era of liturgised law and legalised liturgy' when scribe and priest make the Word of God self-sufficient and independent of God, in the hands of men and a source of idolatry. Ezekiel has a vision of the *'shekinah'* leaving the Temple while the Psalmist proclaims: "We see not signs; there is no longer any prophet".[15] But, then, into this world Jesus Christ was born, the Word made flesh, who dwelt among us, full of grace and truth, God's saving action for Men and Man's perfect obedience to God, the combination of the two aspects of priesthood, to what in fact the whole of the Old Testament had been leading, Christ both the Word and also our Great High Priest. To this St Mary's continues to bear daily witness.

## The Future

It is against this background of history, personal salvation and theology, that St Mary's must face the future. Where are we left in this 125th year of our church's life? We must continue to proclaim the Christian Gospel in terms of both the revelation of God in his Word and in the presentation of this reality in the Liturgy.[16] But, thankfully, the days are gone when Dean Inge, dining at an Oxford high table and asked by the future Cambridge Regius Professor of Divinity, a renowned liturgical scholar, whether he was interested in liturgy, replied: "No; neither do I collect postage stamps."[17] It is the witness of churches such as St Mary's that has made such remarks an impossibility in the 1990s.

There is still space for prophecy, however, for the perversions and distortions that damaged the religion of ancient Israel will damage us too. In the past our priests have spoken with a prophetic voice (as many of the Old Testament priests became prophets, too). Indeed, if they had not it is doubtful if St Mary's would still be here today. Let us pray that they will do so in the future, presenting to us a vision of ourselves, like Israel in the Old Testament, as a kingdom of priests and a holy nation.

Notes

1. One of the more amusing stories associated with these events a generation before the dedication of St Mary's is the accusation that Bennett and his curates were ringing a bell (copying Rome, of course) at the time of the consecration. It turned out that it was in fact the dinner bell of an adjoining house! Both St Barnabas and St Mary's were daughter churches of St Paul's, Knightsbridge, before becoming separate parishes in 1866 and 1909 respectively.

2. Hence the fashionable pejorative description (in the years after Catholic Emancipation, 1829) of the Roman Catholic Church as the 'Italian Mission'. Further historical resonances were made by those who thought of the early English church as a Celtic institution ante-dating the Roman mission of St Augustine.

3. There are parallels in the early history of the Oxford Movement with what has happened in the Church of England of our own day, since 1992 and the ordination of women to the priesthood. Words such as 'authority', 'ecclesiology' and 'apostasy', used today by those who have left the C of E, have a familiar ring for those who have read the documents of the Tractarian Revival.

4. This period in the history of the Oxford Movement strikes an odd note with us today. The issues at stake (principally because the battles were subsequently won) do not seem to be of great importance. But, ritualism represented a necessary public platform on and from which to fight for much more in the way of spiritual and social renewal in the Church. At heart ritualists were clothing the rite they were obliged to use (1662) in an effort to assert its traditional character (and perhaps to hide those aspects which were untraditional). This tension between the 'rite' and the doctrinal interpretation of it remains with us today.

5. 'High Church' relates naturally back to the ideas of the 17th century, when the words were first used to describe the tradition which stressed a Catholic interpretation of such matters as the authority of the Church, the centrality of the episcopate and sacramentalism. 'Anglo-Catholic' was also used in the 17th century, but came into its own in the 19th when the early Tractarians issued their Library of Anglo-Catholic Theology (from 1841).

6. During the whole of Paul's lifetime, the Temple sacrifices continued. Only after AD 70 did the Temple rituals cease.

7. A personal reminiscence is of the vicar of the parish from which I was confirmed as a boy (and which would in those days have been called 'Middle-of-the-Road') who used to feed the left-over bits of the communion bread to the birds after the service. (This, I assure you, I did observe, and it was, for that vicar, merely an enactment of the 1552 rubric.) But we are, here, very far indeed

from any sense that there is a real presence of the body and blood of Christ in the sacrament (however defined). It was from this deficient Receptionism that I and others came to embrace the sacramental orthodoxy of Anglo-Catholicism.

8. By one of those ironies this school, built to accommodate the increase in schools' population which came as the result of the raising of the school leaving age, the growth in the birth rate, and the increasing prominence given to secondary education after the Second World War, has now itself gone, to make way for new housing in the wake of the present fall in school rolls which looks like continuing into the next century.

9. With the growth of Catholic worship, the mass as the main Sunday service, regular times for confession, proper honour given to the Mother of God, weekday celebration and other extra-liturgical functions, in parishes where it would have been unthinkable before the Second World War, the eclectic congregations of the old 'shrine' churches in the centres of cities have diminished in size. In St Mary's this has occurred (as in so many other parishes) at the same time as other 'inner-city' problems have arisen and multiplied. In London, however, people are used to travelling long distances on public transport to go to their work place; they seem also prepared to do the same on Sunday morning for mass and on weekdays for other events such as Bible Studies etc in a church where they also meet like-minded people with whom they readily form friendships and build up the community in that place. This has been our experience at St Mary's for a number of years.

10. By New Testament times the Word of God has become personified, in the Person of Christ (John 1.1–14).

11. The semitic root *dbr* gives us three closely related words in Hebrew. The Word (*dabar*) is housed as the Ten Commandments (*debarim*) in the Tabernacle in the Desert or Holy of Holies (the *debir*) after the building of the Temple.

12. Central to the life of St Mary's has been the recitation of the divine office as well as the more obvious daily mass. With the introduction of longer and more varied Biblical readings and 'responsorial' psalms in the mass, attention to the reading of the Bible has become less important for many. But, until very recently, in congregations such as St Mary's, matins and evensong were read by lay people as much as priests. They got through the whole of the Old Testament once a year, the New Testament twice and the psalms once a month. This was achieved through the Book of Common Prayer. The BCP is criticised nowadays for its paucity of scripture appointed to be read in the Holy Communion, but in essence what the BCP was doing was highlighting in two short readings for Sundays and Saints' Days what was principally covered in the divine office. It must be admitted that daily reception of holy communion and priority given to the celebration of mass remain a scandal for many Orthodox Christians as well as Protestants. We need to face this criticism. The pious Orthodox Christian will be unlikely to take the sacrament without a three-day preparation of prayer and fasting. In Ethiopia the preparation is more strict. Our priests in 1999 do not even, any more, follow either the classic Anglican discipline of spending Saturday evening quietly at home preparing for Sunday's liturgy or the Roman Catholic

*Streets of Heaven*

practice of avoiding food and drink after midnight the day before. Instead, they go to parties and clubs. Reception of holy communion is no longer anything special. One communion becomes a thanksgiving for another and a preparation for the next. The moral of this is clear: the Word is assumed, the Cult presumed. Is there a danger signal here, I wonder? There is certainly much repetition in St Mary's worship. Let us trust that it is not all vain.

13. Numbers 8.89 ff.
14. Amos 5.21 ff.
15. Psalm 74.9.
16. In each of the three sections of this article, Word and Sacrament have rightly dominated the discussion. Readers may not know of Fr Walter Hannah's wonderful, fantastical description of a traveller who discovers a remote Christian tribe in Africa, which has been cut off from Western and Orthodox Christianity since shortly after Apostolic times. In the morning our visitor is taken into church and is amazed to see no altar but many, many pulpits. "We," he is told, "preach our daily sermon here. We say mass once a week." The reply is that he says mass daily and preaches once a week. Word and Sacrament indeed!
17. Arthur Couratin, himself a distinguished liturgist at the University of Oxford, used to tell this story with relish.

# To love and linger

## *Priests departed ~ Henry Hely-Hutchinson*

"THOSE WHO CHOOSE to love and linger." These words, spoken by Fr John Gilling in his retirement sermon in 1990, echo James Elroy Flecker's poem *The Dying Patriot*[1] Fr Gilling was the most recent of a long line of priests who did just that at St Mary's, thereby avoiding any (deserved if not expected) promotion to a deanery or suffragan bishopric perhaps. But then, St Mary's has never been an entirely 'respectable' place, at any time in its history, within mainstream established Anglicanism. "And thank God for that!" one can hear the chorus cry. No. St Mary's genius lies elsewhere, not least in the distinguished priests-in-charge and vicars whom God in his wisdom has sent to us, now over a 125 year period.

Where to begin and end, and whom to exclude? This difficult task is made somewhat easier if we confine ourselves, unwillingly, and approach the task through the memorial tablets in the church honouring former long serving curates and incumbents. They are four in number: to Wentworth Beaumont Hankey, John Cyril Howell, Humphrey Whitby and Stephen Langton (plates 19, 20, 21, 24), located by the sacristy door, on the north and south sides of the sanctuary and on the north wall of the Chapel of the Seven Sorrows, and composed variously in Latin and English on copper, wood and stone. Fr Hankey and Fr Whitby each served here for a period of 31 years, Fr Howell for 11 and Fr Langton for 17. This brief survey looks at their reputations as recorded in these memorials, in their obituaries and through anecdotes about them that have come down to us.

Close contact with St Paul's, Knightsbridge was maintained until St Mary's became an independent entity in 1909 and there is a brass memorial tablet next to the sacristy to the long serving vicar, Henry Montagu Villiers (from 1881 to 1908). How much personal interest Fr Villiers took in the welfare of this daughter church is not known, but one may suspect it was considerable, although not on a day to day basis: only after his death did the question of the independence of St Mary's arise.

Fr Villiers sent one Fr Eyton to look after St Mary's in 1874 and, in his turn and within a year, he invited St Paul's new deacon, **Wentworth Beaumont Hankey**[2] to join him. Fr Hankey was to serve his entire priestly ministry at St Mary's, until his death on his birthday, 16th June 1905. A valuable insight into his character comes from an oil painting now in St Mary's presbytery showing a young man of striking good looks, solid, vigorous. He must have made an awesome impression when visiting the poor of St Mary's parish, dressed in frock coat and seated in the parlour, if there was one, top hat resting upturned on his knees.[3]

His immediate successor Fr Howell, and later, Fr Whitby, both testified to the enduring quality of his work: now, nearly 100 years after his death, we can see that he built well, for he served as a example to later parish priests in his pastoral care, his personal life and his teaching ministry. "The most unselfish clergyman in the Church of England" and "saintly" were tributes in obituaries. St Mary's *District Magazine* (and its successor after 1908, the *Parish Magazine*) record verbatim learned sermons preached by Fr Hankey and religious verse he wrote ten or fifteen years earlier.

What form did his ministry take in those far off days in the late 19th century? He devoted many hours to visiting the sick. He prepared and recorded his sermons meticulously. His teaching was admired for its fervour and for its effectiveness. He spent a life of prayer, mingled with all his other activities. He built slowly, deliberately, inexorably: guilds, sewing classes, mothers' meetings, bible classes and instruction. In those early years, too, St Mary's Cricket XI seems to have enjoyed success. There was one early victim at "a private ground, Trouville Road, Clapham" where St Mary's modest 33, including six extras, was sufficient by a margin of 18 to overwhelm their opponents' total of 15, also including six extras; and we cannot forbear to record one other victory, by an innings over *The Daily Telegraph*—St Mary's 201 (top scorer Fr Eyton 36): *Daily*

*Telegraph* 26 and 16: but this was 23 years before the birth of EW Swanton.

The various religious and national controversies and events of the times—Gallicism and Ultramontanism, Infallibility, Old Catholics, the Diamond Jubilee—all produced a response from Fr Hankey: "Do not condemn Henry VIII. God forbid, in whose hands are the hearts of kings" is an example of his incisive teaching postures. A bare statistic in the *Magazine* of 1891 showing the number of Easter communicants for the previous seven years tells its own story—133, 150, 233, 268, 276, 377, 440. Sure foundations indeed.

His learning in medical and other sciences and in general literature together with his fairness, charity and judgement led him to be sought out as consultant by clergy and laity alike, although he never spoke on a public platform and only rarely outside St Mary's. His delivery, it is sad to learn from one obituarist, was "somewhat monotonous" but "his power of antithesis and epigram was exceptional". George Vaizey, writing seventy years after his death, and without quoting his source, portrays him as "...a leader of exceptional ability; his sermons, when read today, are as graphic and apposite as then. He was like St Augustine, forgetting his surroundings, speaking aloud to God hour after hour in St Mary's. People of the streets around and others from afar came to creep up to be near him and to join with him in devotion."

On his death, Lord Halifax[4] observed: "Tender to others, hard on himself." His ministry was indeed a hard act to follow, but he was succeeded by a man whom he had already been working with and had chosen as his assistant priest, **John Cyril Howell**.[5] "An ideal priest" was Lord Halifax's judgement. He was a magnet for those younger priests who tended to mistrust the beneficed clergy, and who sought him out with confidence, trusting in his sure spiritual insight. "He seemed destined to reconcile differences and to bring divergent elements together."

We have several good photographs of Fr Howell (in most he is wearing an overcoat) which attest to his seriousness, his humility and his sincerity, even his intellect, and perhaps his ill health. Yet, it is not easy to discern the character behind the face. His obituaries give us no help. Clearly his personal warmth attracted and held an intense devotion amongst his friends and parishioners—"he had a real love of souls"—but, in the absence of contemporary evidence, an accurate account of his character and personality is hard to establish.

The cause of Christian unity absorbed his thoughts and energies, as it did those of Lord Halifax. "He made St Mary's a centre of Catholic teaching and practice, a home to many who found comfort and help... One address in especial I remember," wrote an anonymous obituarist, "when he spoke of your road through life being full of the echo of closing doors: doors which closed on aspirations, on hopes, on departed friends and past opportunities; and yet through the sad sounds of them all you must persevere, and go on steadily till you reach the door which leads to Life Everlasting."

Never having enjoyed robust health and by his untiring labours for his community, he "fretted the pygmy body to decay":[6] he was operated on—details were not discussed then as openly as now—and died four days later. Before going into hospital, he confided to Fr Maurice Child, assistant priest, that, if he should not survive the operation, "Humphrey Whitby is the man I would like to succeed me." So, for the second time in a generation the parish priest had named his successor.

The ministry of **Edward Otway Humphrey Whitby**[7] embraced the two world wars. It covered, too, the Malines Conversations, the initiative of Lord Halifax, churchwarden from 1909 until 1934, the great controversies over the new Prayer Book in 1927 and 1928, and the abdication crisis of 1936. There was plenty to keep a fluent commentator at his desk.

Then there were the *Quarterlies*. In 29 successive editions in the 1930s, some 4000 words each, Fr Whitby wrote letters to a young man entitled "Instructions in the Christian Religion" and which only ended with the outbreak of war in 1939 with these words: "Well goodbye, John, for the present and good luck!"

As his photo taken late in life shows, his appearance was stern. Always happier in male company, he remained shy, particularly with women on brief acquaintance, although he did have several great friends of the opposite sex. Overall, however, he allowed his personal relationships to develop slowly. When visiting parishioners he was noted more for his taciturnity, allowing his presence to speak more loudly than mere words. He travelled abroad as frequently as possible: he had a considerable private fortune, bestowing endless benefactions upon St Mary's—vestments, paintings, the endowment of St Mary's Trust, contributions to the work of Goodhart-Rendell, particularly in the building of the Seven Sorrows chapel and the presbytery.

Fr Whitby was a man of many parts. Brian O'Brien[8] deals with his publishing ventures, through the Society of St Peter and St Paul (SSPP). Fr Young[9] describes HW's affection for the Book of Common Prayer, his regard for Cranmer and his unceasing concern for the Church of England. In his obituary Fr Child tells of a visit he and Fr Whitby made together to the Church of the Holy Sepulchre in Jerusalem, where they were assailed by the many other rites proceeding all around—Copts shouting, Syrians bellowing, Armenians rattling handbells, the Orthodox exquisite unaccompanied chanting and Catholic ritual music. "Yes," said Fr Whitby, after some moments' reflection, "the point is that they are all doing something mysterious with bread and wine."

The red, circular, stained glass window over the reredos above the Seven Sorrows altar (designed by Margaret Rope to replace one blown out during the Second World War), is also placed there in his memory. In spite of the numerous and munificent gifts and endowments made during his lifetime, his estate totalled no less than £135,000 at his death. Unlike his predecessors, he did not name the man who was to follow him. The trustees of the Trust he had established to safeguard St Mary's finances and independence were as well the patrons of the living. Their choice proved unusual but inspired.

**Frederick Edward Palmer Stephen Langton**[10] came to St Mary's in his maturity, at the age of 50, and after 17 years in Clerkenwell, then a very poor parish where his attendance amongst those sheltering in the Tube stations and to the injured and dying in the Blitz is remembered with gratitude to this day. He had joined up during the First World War at the age of 18. His plane crashed and he fell out of it, sustaining appalling injuries which hospitalised him for a year and which were responsible for the ill health and pain which dogged him for the rest of his life. He was marvellous with the sick and with children and started a 10am Family Mass which rivalled the High Mass in popularity and was sometimes conducted facing the people, with a Nave Altar: all this in the 1950s, well before Vatican II. Equally popular, with both parents and children, were the Saturday morning 'Gin and Jelly' parties when the children would be entertained by Fr Langton's collection of wind up toys.

Fr Langton was accompanied to St Mary's by a housekeeper, Emma, with her chickens, which took over the garden situated under the bridge from the choir room to the organ loft. Emma deserves a monograph to herself: she had joined Fr Langton after being an outspoken servant at a London convent, where an altercation resulted in her throwing a knife at the Reverend Mother. We get some understanding of Fr Langton through his response to this incident. "She's the one for me!" he decided, and she was to remain with him until the day he died.

St Mary's was faced with post war reconstruction, repairs which had been postponed, damage to east windows from bomb blast, bank balance low and a congregation wary of change after Fr Whitby's long ministry. Against this background of secular concerns, he was a notable confessor and penitents both lay and clerical flocked to him for guidance. "He was never stern," describes one such penitent, "taking the view that any departure from the penitent's rule of life was a failure, a breakdown, in his contract with God." Yet he joked and enjoyed life. He recalled being taken to lunch at the Grosvenor Hotel by Fr Whitby, whose family had owned the hotel, and who was greeted by an old retainer there, "And how are you, Master Humphrey?"

Arthritis struck in his later years. In his last months he was practically immobile. He was a lifelong friend of Robert Mortimer who was Bishop of Exeter and, like Fr Langton, an expert on canon law. They had a pact whereby the survivor would preach at the other's funeral, on the text:

> *They told me, Heraclitus, they told me you were dead*
>
> *They brought me bitter news to hear, and bitter tears to shed.*

and so it was that at Fr Langton's funeral the bishop recalled:

> *I wept as I remembered how often you and I*
>
> *Had tired the sun with talking and sent him down the sky.*

His was a solid ministry, based on a deep personal faith, and giving rise to exceptional devotion amongst his parishioners. He is remembered as someone who had a great love for people, great fun, a wonderful conversationalist with a wicked sense of humour,[11] a good, kindly, old fashioned catholic priest. "Keep the torch burning: pass it on," says the song. This he did. One of his especial legacies was to have invited Dr Eric Mascall to live in the presbytery on his appointment to King's College, London, and whose presence was to prove of great benefit to both the next two vicars, Fr Nicholson and Fr Gilling, and to their congregations.

We have come a long way from 1874 and reached the 1960s, a time when the (often painful) religious changes associated with liturgical renewal, Pope John XXIII's *aggiornamento* and Vatican II (let alone the parallel transformation of society and its values) needed to be faced. What had appeared to be immutable in the practice of the catholic religion was to prove the very opposite.

But that is another tale and concerns the living not the departed, as we pursue our journey upon 'the streets where the great men go'.[12]

Notes

1. Noon strikes on England, noon on Oxford town,
   —Beauty she was statue cold—there's blood upon her gown:
   Noon of my dreams, O noon!
     Proud and godly kings had built her, long ago,
     With her towers and tombs and statues all arow,
   With her fair and floral air and the love that lingers there,
     And the streets where the great men go.
2. Wentworth Beaumont Hankey was born 1848 and died in 1905. He was educated at Eton, Christ Church and Cuddesdon.

*Streets of Heaven*

1.

Exterior of St Mary's from Graham Street in 1874.

Probably based on a sketch by Withers, this shows the church much as it remains today.
Note the small vestry as it was before Goodhart-Rendel's extension.

2.

Interior of St Mary's in 1874.

The picture shows the original
admired reredos and altar and
the decorated brickwork,
which Goodhart-Rendel liked,
before the paintings were
added. The ceiling decoration
can still be discerned today
under the thick varnish. Note
the stone chancel wall and
pulpit on the north side of the
steps.

3.
Interior of St Mary's in the 1880s?

An accurate water colour, which shows the painting of the Annunciation and the stained glass windows already in place. The stone pulpit is still on the north but the stone wall has been replaced with a very fine wrought iron screen, part of which can still be seen on the south side of the altar of the Seven Sorrows.

4.
Reredos by S. Gambier Parry c.1909.

Considering its supposed date it is surprisingly in an Elizabethan style. Note the
strapwork cresting with the IHS sunburst. The arch, shorn of its decoration, with its
related pilaster can still be seen in the reredos today, see plate 7.

5.

The organ case by S. Gambier Parry c1908–1913.

A fine example of the then fashionable Wren baroque revival, with Grinling Gibbonsesque carving. To its rear can just be seen the window of 1897 by Miss Lowndes.

6.

'*Pictures of the English Liturgy Volume 1 High Mass*' Martin Travers 1916.

An example of Travers' revival of a Tridentine sarcophagus shaped high altar, very similar to his design for St Mary's.

7.

A fashionable wedding at St Mary's in the late 1920s.

This shows the high altar and reredos as Martin Travers left them. The strapwork cresting and the arch still remain from Gambier Parry's design, Goodhart Rendel's cresting and great volutes to either side have yet to be fixed, but the tabernacle, the rococo gradine and the baroque candle sticks are already there as is Travers' magnificent Festival front.

8.
Preliminary design for the cresting to the reredos by Goodhart-Rendel dated 4.4.34.

This is a proposal by Goodhart-Rendel in the Travers style to replace Parry's Elizabethan cresting. Goodhart-Rendel produced an extraordinary baroque sunburst containing an oval recess with sculpture showing the Coronation of the Virgin; which in its final design is capped with volutes that suggest an early 18th century wig.

9.
Our Lady of Peace. designed and carved (?) by Martin Travers, 1920.

A magnificent and completely original war memorial appropriately based on the mediaeval statue at Amiens, well known to the soldiers of the Great War, but here given a baroque twist by Travers' gold and silver leaf.

10.
Looking through Goodhart–Rendel's north aisle to the High Altar today.

Goodhart–Rendel's astyler granite columns flank the view to the combined Parry/Travers/Goodhart–Rendel High Altar and reredos. To the right can be seen Goodhart–Rendel's gothic re-revival St John the Baptist's altar.

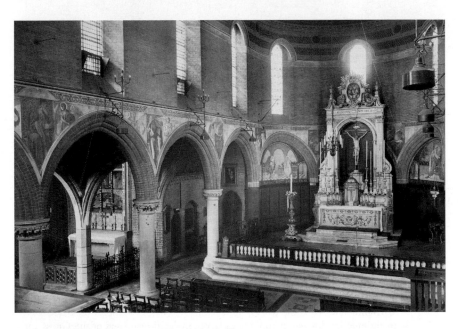

11.
Interior of church looking from the west, above the organ loft, towards the Seven Sorrows altar.

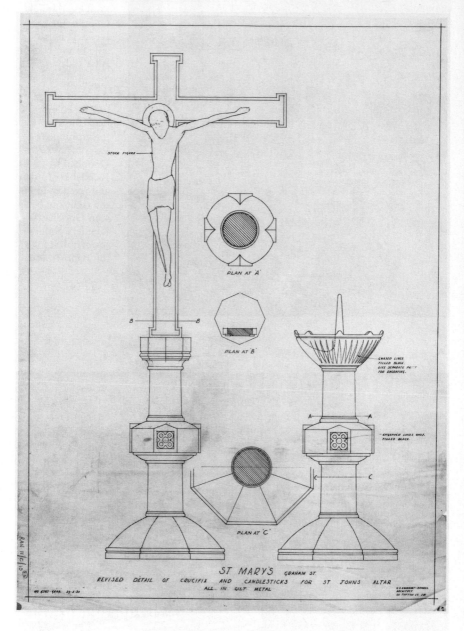

ST MARYS GRAHAM ST.
REVISED DETAIL OF CRUCIFIX AND CANDLESTICKS FOR ST JOHNS ALTAR
ALL IN GILT METAL

12.
Seven Sorrows altar. Design for candle sticks and crucifix: Goodhart-Rendel dated 29.3.30.

This is an early design for the splendid lapis lazuli, malachite and red enamel cross and candle sticks which have all the glamour and modernity of smart 1920s jewellery.

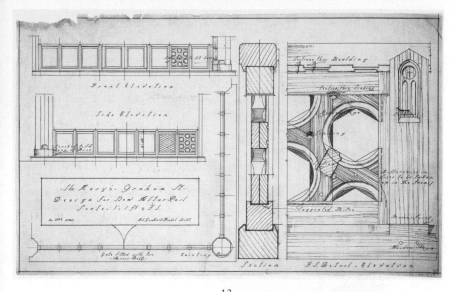

13.

Seven Sorrows chapel. Design for altar rails: Goodhart-Rendel dated ???

Built by the fashionable furniture maker Betty Joel. Note the clever use of simple interlocking timber pieces which create an intricate pattern. In fact only the altar rails to the front of the chapel were made, on the south side part of the early wrought iron main altar rails were fixed.

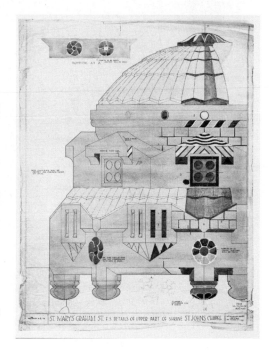

14.
St John the Baptist chapel detail of domed tabernacle top; Goodhart-Rendel dated 22.XI.29

A most remarkable example of extremely early Re-revival of Victorian design, in this case in the manner of William Burges, though Goodhart-Rendel's colouring has little of Burges' intensity of colouring. Goodhart-Rendel is much influenced by such contemporary sources as Bakst and the Russian ballet.

15.
Proposed tower over a
large narthex. Perspective
by Goodhart-Rendel.

Based on Norman Shaw's
great saddle back tower
to his church in Lyon of
1869. Unbuilt, but had it
been built on the site of
Bell House (26 Graham
St.) it would have given a
great narthex and choir
gallery to the church and
would have dominated
the whole of south
Pimlico, though ironically
it might well not have
survived the bombing of
Sloane Square station.

16.
The Seven Sorrows altar as it was before the Goodhart-Rendel
reredos was installed in 1929.

17.
Looking through Goodhart-Rendel's north aisle to the
Gambier Parry organ loft today.

18.
Part of the High Mass set designed by
Martin Travers for Fr Whitby in 1911.

19.
Fr W Beaumont Hankey, curate 1874–1905.

20.
Fr Cyril Howell, first parish priest 1909–1916.

21.
Fr Humphrey Whitby, parish priest 1916–1948.

22.
Vicount Halifax, church warden 1909–1934.

23.
Fr Maurice Child, assistant priest 1917–1923; Fr Humphrey Whitby parish priest 1916–1948 and Fr Audley Brown.

24.
Fr Stephen Langton, parish priest 1948–1964.

3. Cicely Paget Bowman, churchwarden of St Mary's from 1996 to 1999, came to live in Chester Row in 1938 and was given this reminiscence by an elderly member of the congregation at that time.
4. Charles Lindley, 2nd Viscount Halifax (1839–1934).
5. John Cyril Howell was born in 1872 and died in 1916. He came to St Mary's from St Mary's Paddington and became St Mary's first vicar in 1909.
6. Dryden, *Absalom and Achitophel*.
7. Edward Otway Humphrey Whitby was born in 1883 and died in 1948. He became Vicar in 1916, retiring through ill health in 1947. He was educated at Radley and University College, Oxford. Ordained deacon in 1910 and priest a year later, he came to us from St Columba, Haggerston where he had served with Fr Maurice Child (who was also a curate at St Mary's and became Fr Whitby's obituarist). He is buried at All Saints, Wyke Regis.
8. See page 97.
9. See page 100.
10. Frederick Edward Palmer Stephen Langton was born in 1897 and died in 1972. After St John's College, Cambridge he was ordained in 1924 but he had before that served in the Royal Flying Corps and HW reflected, upon hearing him named as his successor, that he must have witnessed his valour in the air combats over London during the Great War. He served curacies at St Michael's, Shoreditch and St Cuthbert's, Philbeach Gardens before being appointed vicar of Holy Redeemer, Clerkenwell in 1931 where he served until 1948, including the war years.
11. His was this parody of the famous hymn:
Onward Christian soldiers
Marching as to war
With the Cross of Jesus
Left behind the door!
12. See note 1.

# Good and faithful servants

## *St Mary's Trust ~ David Marchese*

ST MARY'S TRUST is a registered charity which holds the principal fund for the benefit of St Mary's church. St Mary's has had trustees since first becoming a separate parish in 1909, when the Bishop of London made it a condition of allowing the parish to be formed that the sum of £5,000 should be raised and settled on trustees in order to make St Mary's financially independent. The trustees, amongst whom was Lord Halifax, were also granted the patronage or right to appoint the vicar.

By 1922, when Fr Humphrey Whitby was vicar, it appears that the original trust fund had been used up, probably as a result of the First World War. At the same time, plans were afoot to expand the church buildings in response to the growing popularity of St Mary's. Furthermore, the parish had no parsonage house to accommodate the clergy.

Fortunately, Fr Whitby was not only devoted to St Mary's but also a man of private means. He generously endowed the church, by purchasing in 1922 from the Duke of Westminster's Grosvenor Estate the neighbouring properties of 28, 29 and 30 Bourne Street (then called Westbourne Street) and 26 Graham Terrace, which was originally intended to be pulled down in order to build a bell tower. The land on which 28 and 29 Bourne Street stood was used to build the Seven Sorrows chapel and a new entrance to the church in Bourne Street. It was subsequently transferred (in the usual way) to the Church Commissioners. Number 30 Bourne Street, an imposing public house known as "The Pineapple", was converted into a new presbytery to house the vicar and two curates.

Under the 1922 conveyance by which these properties were acquired, they were settled on trustees for the benefit of St Mary's. In the following year, 1923, St Mary's Trust itself was set up. The trustees were the same as those appointed under the 1922 conveyance, and they were also entrusted with the right of patronage.

The Trust Deed recites that: "The Trustees with the approval of [Fr] Whitby have constituted a Fund under the name of 'St Mary's Trust'... to which certain contributions... have already been made... and it is expected that further contributions will from time to time hereafter be made to the Fund to the same extent." The purpose and objects of the Trust were stated (in the same terms as those under the 1922 Conveyance) to be that: "The Trustees shall pay or apply the income and/or capital of the Fund in such manner for such legally charitable purposes in connection with or for the benefit of the Church of St Mary the Virgin Graham Street aforesaid or the work of the Church of England in the Parish of St Mary the Virgin aforesaid or in the neighbourhood of that Parish as the trustees in their absolute discretion shall from time to time think fit."

The establishment of the Trust, coupled with the right of patronage, must have been regarded as a vital safeguard to ensure that the Anglo-Catholic tradition in which St Mary's had developed since its founding in 1874 would be free from possibly hostile interference by the authorities. The founders of the Trust would have been all too aware of the difficulties, even persecution, which Catholics in the Church of England had suffered in the 19th century, when St Barnabas' church down the road had been the scene of anti-ritualistic riots. There was always the possibility that the ecclesiastical authorities, present or future, would not be sympathetic to St Mary's, because of its churchmanship, its aims of reunion with Rome, and the type of services it maintained. St Mary's has never been a typical parish, having a small parochial area and a congregation drawn from diverse areas and walks of life. That has undoubtedly added to the richness and vitality of its communal life. But the possibilities of change, and the desirability of continuity, must have been in the minds of the founders of the Trust when they established it as a discretionary trust, with wide and general powers.

The 1922 conveyance contained an express power for the acquired properties to be used "for a Clergy House... or for the accommodation of any persons (of either sex) for the time being attached to or working in connection with the said Church", and one of the chief functions of the trustees over the years has been the upkeep of the presbytery. In due course, when sisters were attached to the parish, the annexe to the presbytery known as 'the cottage' was provided for them, and subsequently for the sacristan, Anne Mundy.

Originally the presbytery was a strictly private residence, but over the course of time the large 'public' rooms have become more and more used for parish functions. In the 1920's the Carmel Hall in Bourne Street (originally a non conformist chapel) had been acquired as a parish hall for St Mary's, but in the post-war period it was disposed of. So, again unlike other parishes, St Mary's does not have a parish hall, and in many ways the presbytery now fulfils this function. What was at one time the vicar's private study on the ground floor has in recent years been turned into a parish office for the use of our parish administrator.

In addition to a third-floor flat which until 1999 was the vicar's residence, the presbytery contains two small flats on the second floor which were originally used by the curates, and in the course of time by honorary assistant priests who assist with the work of St Mary's, and who have included the late Dr Eric Mascall.

Following what is known as the Sheffield Report, it has for some time been the policy of the Church of England not to allow assistant curates to be appointed to a parish unless there is a demonstrable need. When Fr Bill Scott became vicar in 1992, it was clear that he would not be able to appoint another curate, and in 1993 the last full time assistant curate (Fr Nicholas Kavanagh) left to become part of a team ministry in Brighton. However, in 1997 Fr Scott became priest-in-charge of St Barnabas, Pimlico and area dean, and for this reason he was permitted to appoint Fr Nick Mercer as a full-time assistant curate.

It was a condition of the appointment that the new curate should be accommodated through the parish's own financial resources. There was no room left in the presbytery, and it had by then become apparent that the accommodation provided for the vicar of St Mary's did not meet the standards set by the Church Commissioners.

The trustees therefore decided to exercise their right to recover 26 Graham Terrace, which had been previously let, in order to provide a residence for the vicar, and so to enable the new curate to reside in what had previously been the vicar's flat in the presbytery. Eventually, legal possession of the house was recovered in 1998, and after considerable repair and refurbishment (in part with the aid of the Hyde Park Place Estate Charity and a donor who wishes to remain anonymous) Fr Scott was able to take up residence in early 1999.

St Mary's Trust, like other charitable funds, has a portfolio of investments—government stocks and quoted stocks and shares—which provide its main income. The trust fund has expanded over the years, partly because of donations and legacies received from time to time, and partly through the management of its investments on the advice of the Trust's brokers. Details of the investments, and the income and expenditure of the Trust, are set out in the annual accounts, which are exhibited in church. The unusually high expenditure in 1998 on the repair and refurbishment of 26 Graham Terrace and the presbytery will inevitably affect the Trust's future annual income. For a number of years from the 1970s to the early 1990s, members of the congregation were encouraged to make covenants with the Trust to satisfy their stewardship obligations, although more funds were actually paid out of the Trust to the parish than were ever contributed by way of covenants. Nowadays all covenanting is directly with the parochial church council. The Trust has its own running expenses, of course, but most of its income has always been applied for the benefit of St Mary's.

The work of the trustees continues with the three rôles of exercising the right of patronage, accommodating the parish clergy, and providing financial support for parish activities. Nowadays, the right of patronage is subject to the veto of the parish representatives as well as the bishop. It is of course not possible for a parochial church council to be the patron of a living, but having the patronage vested in parish trustees avoids possibly unsympathetic outsiders exercising this function. Otherwise the trustees of St Mary's Trust have no special powers or status in relation to St Mary's, and are subject to the normal duties of charitable trustees.

The 'plant' in the care of the trustees, in which the vicar and curate reside, as well as the honorary assistant priests and sacristan, has to be maintained on almost a continuous basis. The presbytery itself houses the boilers which heat the church as well as the domestic accommodation. There is a lift serving the five levels of the presbytery and a dumb waiter to the first-floor dining room, reputedly the oldest installed by The Express Lift Company that are still in working order (officially obsolete but serviceable). The undercroft beneath the presbytery is let out for part of the year to The Victoria School of English, with whom there have always been good relations.

Apart from regular subventions towards the parish deficit (produced by the excess of its expenditure over its income), the trustees have also applied the trust funds from time to time in order to assist with major expenditure of the parish, for example when the organ was restored in 1982. The trustees have always been willing to assist in this way, although their policy has been to encourage the parish to seek ways of funding ordinary expenditure out of current income.

As is usual with a charitable trust, the day-to-day management of St Mary's Trust is delegated to a managing trustee, but major decisions are taken by the trustees as a whole. Charitable trustees, unlike ordinary trustees, are allowed by law to take majority decisions, but usually a consensus emerges on any major decision. The work of the managing trustee involves liaising with the Trust's stockbrokers, bankers, accountants, solicitors, architects and insurers, as well as surveyors, builders and other service providers. Records must be maintained, papers have to be collated for submission to the accountants so that they can prepare the annual accounts, tax claims have to be pursued with the Inland Revenue, and annual returns have to be made to the Charity Commission. The work of the trustees is, of course, voluntary and unpaid.

St Mary's Trust provides relatively secure and independent financial assistance for the work and life of the church. Precisely because it is discretionary, its assets cannot be attacked as ecclesiastical property. The wide range of its objects means that, within the terms of its founding Trust Deed and charity law, it is not limited in the ways its funds may be applied to the same extent that a more restricted local trust fund would be. The patronage, now exercised in conjunction with the parish representatives, gives security for the tradition which St Mary's seeks to pass on to future generations. St Mary's Trust was founded in Christian love and generosity, and is something for we should be proud and thankful.

# The same but different

*Recent decades ~ Fr Bill Scott*

WE ARE the pilgrim people of God and not keepers of a museum. This bold statement is one with which all my predecessors would have agreed and to which the continuance of St Mary's in this rather godless age bears so me witness. Henry Hely-Hutchinson in "To love and linger"[1] has brought us the story of St Mary's through the eyes of its priests in charge and vicars up to the 1960s. I would like to extend this story up to the present day, partly from hearsay about the past and party from my own experience.

To remember with any vividness the 1960s we have to be part of an older generation. Although I was 14 in 1960, I was not altogether in tune with the revolutionary times. I am reminded of Philip Larkin's words:

*So life was never better than*
*In nineteen sixty-three*
*(Though just too late for me)—*
*Between the end of the* Chatterly *ban*
*And the Beatles' first LP.*[2]

I must confess that, along with many St Mary's people, despite my fragile age, the brave new world of the 1960s had arrived "just too late for me". Not simply the sexual revolution but the *aggiornamento* of Pope John XXIII, the Second Vatican Council, the changes to age old ceremonies, customs and attitudes did not arrive without many of us feeling very threatened. When Canon Donald Nicholson became parish priest in 1964 he promised to "change nothing" for at least a year. The pace of events overtook him and he was immediately faced with a choice—to keep St Mary's as a museum and observe ritual from which Catholic Christendom had moved on, or to change. He was soon introducing liturgical innovations. Although it was undoubtedly unpleasant at the time, we owe a great debt of gratitude to Canon Nicholson for rather selflessly making us realise that we were part of the pilgrim church.

When Fr John Gilling arrived in 1971 to begin a long and outstanding incumbency, he consolidated what he inherited and brought his own artistic and academic ways to flower. If we think of St Mary's liturgy we think of a rather grand, somewhat conservative rite. However, if the High Mass were performed now in the same way that it was in 1963, I think we should be rather surprised, somewhat amused and probably shocked! What we have today bears continuing witness to the brilliance of both my predecessors in choosing to modernise the liturgy and not hang on to museum-piece ceremonial, to develop the preaching ministry, and to conserve what is good and uplifting. Little is done which is not in line with Roman Catholic ceremonial instructions, and, therefore, western catholic tradition. When it comes to the words in Cranmerian English we may seem more museum-like, but they are still an authorised use in the Church of England and can still, I believe, be a vehicle to lift the mind and heart to God in a way which many of the modern translations do not. In the music, as Shane Fletcher our Master of Music always reminds me, there is great variety—Benjamin Britten and Palestrina with a bit of Mozart for good measure. We sit, therefore, in a halfway house between ancient and modern, very definitely reflecting catholic liturgy, but with a traditional face. St Mary's in the 1990s is, therefore, "the same but different."

The theme of the pilgrim church can easily be eroded with the stability of the parish church, with the collecting of things, albeit beautiful things, from the past and by using music in the culture of a different age. This publication naturally reflects our usage and our possessions and our rather conservative attitudes. Timothy Ashurst and Roderick Gradidge write on the glories of the eucharistic vestments and on the architectural setting.[3] They stir up in us a desire to appreciate the building and its contents more and more, and to admire and wonder at the skill which was used in creating them, and to cheer at the idea of using only the best for God. Do they, however, have any purpose in our Christian pilgrimage? I have often thought it rather strange that in the Christian tradition we 'find' God in a temple created by human beings. Surely God is to be found rather in something of his own creation.

In the Old Testament story of Jacob dreaming and wrestling with God he exclaims, "How awesome is this place! This is none other than the house of God and the gate of heaven." Having found this place he kept going back to it, as did his children for generations. Their focus was the big stone Jacob had set up, anointed and called the house of God. Is God not rather in the beauty of the mountains or in the glory of the sky at night? That stone was the place where God was at home with Jacob. When he fled through the desert from Esau he was aware of the vastness of the created world around him in the wind and the rocks and the gleaming sky. What the frightened man needed to know was that God would come along and be with him in a homely sort of way! Bethel was Jacob's place of security.

It is not too great a leap to say that one of the great features of St Mary's is that so many people find here a home—a place to be at home with God and feel secure, uplifted and enabled for the roughness of life 'in the world.' The building and the ornaments are there to celebrate that God is at home with us and we with him. Jacob met with the mercy of God. We know God in the "substance of our mortal flesh" and "born of the Virgin Mary." Unlike Jacob we have no need to go to actual historical spots, Bethlehem or Calvary, because he is present in every mass, the precious Body stored in the tabernacle. "The word became flesh and dwelt among us." (St John 1) St Mary's as a eucharistic centre with the tabernacle at the heart and the frequent offering of the mass is indeed the place where God meets with his pilgrim people leading them onwards. The mass is not simply a visual aid to a dying Christ, but the effective sign of a living Lord. Every weekday mass is offered twice, alongside the divine office and on Sundays and holy days every opportunity is given to take part in the eucharistic offering.

The other way that we make ourselves at home with the merciful one is through the Sacrament of Reconciliation. This tends nowadays to be a rather hidden ministry because, except before festivals, there are few queues. Not a week goes past, however, without a number of confessions being made and reconciliation taking place—a returning home to the same welcome as did the prodigal son. A church building is a consecrated space—a space into which God has been invoked in a specific way. It is a space where we can be at home and see ourselves as we are, in relationship with God. A church building should bring us to our knees, because the prayer seems to enter the very stones.

> You are not here to verify,
> Instruct yourself, or inform curiosity
> Or carry report. You are here to kneel
> Where prayer has been valid.[4]

The architectural furnishings, the beauty of the worship, the eucharistic presence, the relaxed ceremonial and the prayers of those who have gone before us all add up to St Mary's being a place where prayer is valid. It does not seem unnatural or strange to lift the heart and mind to God in these surroundings. In this way our vocation as pilgrim people continues and we go forward into the next millennium and the next period of our life in faith and hope. Within the daily round of prayer and sacrament there have been landmarks on our pilgrim way.

The missionising inspiration of Fr Gilling, who on accepting the living made it a condition that there should be a full scale mission to Pimlico, blossomed two years after the centenary (1974) in 1976. During the week-long mission, Fr Harry Williams CR led a lunch-time school of prayer later published as *Becoming What I Am* (DLT, 1977). There were evening meetings with entertainment, dancing and harpsichord playing and preaching by Canon Gonville ffrench-Beytagh. Every house in the parish was visited twice by teams of people who met regularly before the actual mission to pray and plan: some 60 to 70 people in all. A few years later another mission called 'A Diamond in Pimlico' was led by the the late Canon David Diamond of St Paul's, Deptford. In the early 1970s the Parish Pilgrimages to Walsingham were not gentle affairs as they are today. Priests, servers, vestment and musicians—indeed the whole ethos of St Mary's was transported to Norfolk.

From 1983–91, St Mary's published six books under the series title *Tracts for Our Times*, the first commemorating the 150th anniversary of the Oxford Movement, and these sold throughout the world.

In 1983 the Community of the Sacred Passion (CSP) withdrew their Sisters from St Mary's—the first time in over 100 years that nuns had not been working and resident in the parish. Fr Gilling made efforts to replace them from other Communities but, perhaps due to a shortage of vocation among the young, he was unsuccessful. He envisaged a new beginning and offered the position of sacristan to Anne Mundy, the head server's wife, thus spreading the Sisters' work over a wider field.

The 1980s was an active time in the life of St Mary's. Parish retreats were a regular event and so were visits to Walsingham where, in 1984, we were enrolled as a member of the Walsingham Cell. Weekly discussion meetings were held during which biblical topics were discussed and Fr Gilling (or the curate) would invite eminent theologians to speak. The members of the congregation were divided into 'House Groups' with the aim of encouraging friendliness and deepening the faith of all involved. They met publicly and socially, arranging house masses, discussion groups, hospital visits and even visits to the theatre. The two main Groups were very successful and were nicknamed the 'Hares' and the 'Tortoises'. The latter still meets and has grown in numbers.

Another development in Fr Gilling's day was his becoming chaplain to the local Francis Holland School—a position I have inherited. This led to the school worshipping in the church and to several good connections with students present and past. There is a school mass several times a term and, just recently, the whole school from infants to sixth form crammed in for the school birthday service. I still visit every week and take part in confirmation preparation.

Having arrived in 1991 and brought the congregation together for a very successful parish day from which emanated many good ideas, a momentous event happened in November 1992. The

Church of England decided to allow women to be ordained to the ministerial priesthood. I have my own views on this subject but unlike many of my friends, I decided that I had to remain within the Church of England and help others to do the same. The PCC decided that women priests would not function at St Mary's neither would a woman incumbent be appointed. Some 40 members of St Mary's congregation decided to leave and become Roman Catholics. This was a painful time for many people on both sides of the debate but my own instinct was to stay and pray. God has seen fit to send us many new members of the congregation so that our numbers are greater that in 1992. One of the bright spots, albeit a modest one, has been the re-instatement of a children's mass and sunday school. This has a committed and growing number of young people who arrange visits and outings to interesting places.

After several years of talking and planning, the Church Commissioners published a scheme to unite the benefice of St Barnabas, Pimlico with St Mary's. This fell at the last post because there seemed to be too many objections on both sides. In September 1997, however, I was licensed as priest in charge of that parish and also as area dean of Westminster (St Margaret). In the loving kindness of the diocesan authorities an assistant priest, Fr Nick Mercer was appointed. He is now part of our family and brings with him many gifts and much experience. Just before my appointment, John Greenhalgh was appointed as full-time parish administrator and verger. He had been part-time verger for many years. He too has made his mark on our parish life and takes care of many things with great flair for which I am very grateful. The backdrop to all this remains the continuing life of a pilgrim people in a place where God is brought closer to humanity and humanity to God through daily mass.

Notes
1. "To love and linger", pp 44–51
2. Philip Larkin, "Annus mirabilis".
3. "Garments of Salvation", pp 104–113; "A very ordinary church", pp 67–86.
4. TS Eliot, "Little Gidding".

# Part II

# Joys and Sorrows

*Worship and Practice*

# A very ordinary church

## *An architectural history of St Mary's ~ Roderick Gradidge*

"**S**T MARY'S is really a very ordinary church—it is in reality typical of hundreds of low-price red-brick gothic churches that were put up in the 1870s and '80s, in London and all over the country. But the impression it makes on the casual visitor or the new worshipper is far from ordinary. How well I remember my first visit! Some friends of mine had taken rooms in Graham Terrace, and I wandered in one day to look at the church. It was like straying into another world—or, at least into another country; I was immediately struck by the soft, remote daylight, by the coolness, the mysterious dark corners, by the stillness (broken every so often by the rumble of an underground train,) and by the rich glow of gilded furnishings against red-brick walls. It was an experience akin to entering such churches as San Zanipolo or the Frari, in Venice—despite the difference in scale; and this, I suppose, was the effect it was intended to have…

"The faded gilt of the ornaments stands out—against the mellow red brick; but there is a deliberate almost naughty pursuit of incongruity in mixing gothic and neo-classical and renaissance and baroque, all in the interests of suggesting that the church has grown slowly over the centuries. It is this which more than anything produces the sensation of having walked into a Catholic church that has always a been Catholic church…

"There has been a deliberate attempt to make you 'feel at home' in St Mary's; and this is, at least in part, achieved by the sensitive use of essentially domestic styles and details. Not, perhaps, the style of everybody's home; but, surely, the style of those houses in Belgravia from which people would come to St Mary's? There is very little in St Mary's of the specially designed 'ecclesiastical' furnishings that make other churches seem so dull and conventional; the polished wood-work, the gilded gesso—even the wood block flooring of the sanctuary—combine to suggest a private house

---

of unusual sumptuousness; and one, of course, that has been continuously lived in by the same family over many generations." (Brian Brindley, *Infinite Riches in a Little Room*, pp 2, 3 and 4.)

The contrast between the simple and austere exterior and the combined splendour of the gilding of Martin Travers' baroque and the sophisticated late gothic revival of Goodhart-Rendel, is something unique in the Anglican church today. But, as Canon Brindley (as he then was) points out, it is the quality of enclosure and warmth that wraps you as you enter (so that you are almost forced on your knees) that makes St Mary's so very special. It is something that it did not have 125 years ago, when it was new, but something that has been created by a series of remarkable priests and designers both through their prayer and their talent. The architectural history of the church falls into five parts, the first four dominated by individual designers.

## RJ Withers (1823–1904)

St Mary's was built in 1873–4 by an obscure church architect, RJ Withers, a pupil of the equally obscure Thomas Hellyer. Withers is hardly known since his work is not particularly distinguished and he did most of it in the West Country, including a school at Poyntington, Dorset in 1848; St Mary's, Llanfair Nantgwyn, Pembroke in 1859, and Cardigan Municipal Buildings in 1859–60. In 1862–5 he designed the Anglican Church of the Resurrection in Brussels. In London that year he restored the post-Reformation fittings in St Ethelburga's, Bishopsgate (this work was removed by Comper in 1912, which in its turn was recently removed by an IRA bomb) and in 1871 he made alterations in St Mary-le-Strand. In 1874, whilst also designing St Mary's, he rearranged the chancel of St Barnabas, Homerton High Street, and extended St James, Norland Square. In 1880 he designed, but only built the temporary nave of, St John the Divine, Balham. More importantly in 1859–60 he built the offices and workshops of the church decorators Lavers and Barraud in Endell Street, Covent Garden, which still exist.

Oddly enough his brother, FC Withers had a similar career in New York, designing a number of small and not particularly distinguished churches, including the Church of the Transfiguration, East 29th Street, of 1849–61, 'the little church around the corner'. From the dedication of these churches he would seem to be more high church than his English brother.

The reason why the very obscure Withers was chosen to design St Mary's is explained by the fact that in 1870 he took over the work at the famous high church of St Paul, Knightsbridge, where he made a number of alterations to Cundy's church of 1840, including new altar steps, choir seats and a reredos of stone alabaster and mosaic. All this was swept away by GF Bodley's much more radical and finer alterations in 1891. Only Withers' porch survives. But interestingly the fine east window, and other windows, are by Lavers and Westlake, (which the firm became after 1868). Presumably they were commissioned because of the Withers connection, or was it possibly the other way around? Did Lavers recommend Withers to St Paul's?

What is certain is that St Mary's is St Paul's daughter church, and was designed at the time that Withers was architect to St Paul's. Not one of the great Victorian architects, he probably seemed suitable for lowly Pimlico, for the servants of the wealthy congregation living in Knightsbridge and Eaton Square. The unnamed author of *St Mary's Pimlico, A Sketch of a Little Church now Fifty Years Old* (SSPP, 1924), describes the site when St Mary's was built. "It was hardly safe to venture after dusk into the network of slums and mean streets between Chelsea Barracks and Sloane Square, two of the most notorious of which were called George Street and The Ditch. These undesirable purlieus are now replaced by the handsome red brick houses of Sloane Gardens and Lower Sloane Street."

And that is the reason why it was not long before St Mary's ceased to be a 'servants' church' and became extremely fashionable. The author of the 1924 pamphlet recalls the congregation before the Great War: "It was at the 10.30 Mass that the Catholic-minded members of the congregation assisted; and one remembers among them Lord and Lady Halifax, the late Lord and Lady Ravensworth and their daughters, Lord and Lady Phillimore and their family— Sir John and Lady Riddell, Sir Alfred and Lady Slade, Mrs Duff Gordon and her three sons, General and Mrs Green Wilkinson…"

Withers in his obituary was said to build a "good, cheap type of brick church", which well describes the original St Mary's. From Graham Terrace the church gives no indication of the glory to be found within. Simple low windowless aisles support a tall clerestory, above which a plain slate roof runs, the ridge capped with a simple bell-cote. The most admired designer of this sort of church was James Brooks whose great Anglo-Catholic red brick churches used to dominate the East End. St Mary's, with its apsed chancel and its long straight ridge, is very like the work of Brooks.

Although it was an obscure servants' church, St Mary's was noticed when it was built. In the folio *The Old and New Churches of London* by JM Capes and Alfred Capes Architects, of 1880, after having illustrated the ancient churches of London and most of the great high Victorian masterpieces, there are plates of the elevation and the interior of St Mary's (plates 1 and 2). The caption reads: "St Mary's is another church built within the last few years, and is a good example of the time at which it was built. Its architect was Mr Withers; the style, that of the 13th century. It holds 400 persons. The organ is by Walker. The curate-in-charge is the Revd R Eyton." The plate of the outside shows the Graham Street front very much as it is today.

The interior is very similar to a coloured picture in the presbytery (plate 3). The ceiling is stencilled with the patterns that can still just be discerned under the dark varnish put on some time later (because of the early 20th-century desire to hide any Victorian decoration both here and in any other part of the church). The walls were plain red brick.

Goodhart-Rendel, writing in St Mary's *Quarterly* of 1925, quotes approvingly an early description of the walls of the church. "Most wisely but one colour of brick is used, but monotony is avoided, by the insertion of bricks of various sections, affording little bits of sharp shadow. How vastly superior is this quiet and modest treatment to the many coloured bricks so frequently seen at the present time." Many of these brick projections had been covered in the spandrels to the arches by canvasses by the time Goodhart-Rendel came to St Mary's. The painter of these is not known. They were done in the late 1890s and are very likely to be by Lavers and Westlake, and painted by Westlake. He was an important painter of church murals and continued to work until early in the 20th century. He also wrote important books on church glass and painting. There is no record either of who painted the two lunettes in the sanctuary. We only know that they were given by parishioners of St Paul's as memorials, the Annunciation to the vicar Mr (sic) Liddell and the Visitation to the son of a Mr and Mrs Winn. Is this the same son commemorated in a memorial brass on the first step of the communion rail nearest the shrine of St John the Baptist which reads: "Edmund John Winn, son of Charles and Priscilla Winn of Nostell Priory... this altar rail is dedicated"?

The pulpit is shown on the north side of the chancel wall and there is a gothic reredos with our Lord on the cross with rood figures to either side. Described by the *Church Times* at the time of the opening as "Bold figures of our Lady and St John on either side of the crucifix appear on the reredos, in front of which stands one of the most effective altars we have seen of late. It is formed of sweet cedar and is richly ornamented with gold and colour." Canon Brindley claims that this can still be seen behind Travers' great reredos (op cit p 6). There is no stained glass in the picture, though three stained glass windows were soon put in by the Allcard family of St Paul's, Knightsbridge, but they were blown out in the 1939 war. The seats are not shown so presumably there were never any pews which is in the correct Tractarian tradition. The author of the 1924 pamphlet remembers that "The Sanctuary in former times was much restricted being blocked on either side by a double row of choir stalls. There were also stalls for priests officiating at Mattins and Evensong—anything like a ceremonial choir was, under these circumstances, impossible" (op cit p 7). Although chandelier ring lights are shown in the coloured perspective they are not shown in the print. A wall at the chancel steps is shown but this was no doubt soon done away with, to be replaced with the very fine wrought-iron altar rails, part of which can still be seen on the south side of the Chapel of the Seven Sorrows.

One of the first additions to the church was the west window of 1897 designed by Miss Lowndes of Lowndes and Drury of the King's Road, a firm of lady stained glass artists which survived into the 1980s. It is unfortunately now largely hidden by Gambier Parry's great organ case and little can be seen of it but a red glow in the evening; it has figures of St George and St Edward the Confessor, and is rather fine.

## S Gambier Parry (1859–1948)

Thirty years after the church was built, with the arrival of Fr Howell as curate in 1905 and vicar from 1909 to 1916, important church furnishings started to be added. The first designer involved was as obscure as RJ Withers and also came from the West. S Gambier Parry was the son of the Gloucestershire landowner and inventor of a spirit fresco, T Gambier Parry, who very successfully painted the ceiling of Ely Cathedral, and the nephew of Charles Parry, composer of *Jerusalem* and *Blest Pair of Sirens*. He largely worked in west Gloucestershire and lived in Duntisbourne Rouse with offices in Victoria Street. David Verey in his *Buildings of England: Gloucestershire* describes the two churches that he built at Bentham and Tidenham Chase, both of 1888, as very disappointing, although he prefers the restorations at Cranham and Bulley. All these were in coarse Gothic that does nothing to explain why, at the turn of the century, Gambier Parry should have turned to the Wren style, except that it was a style that was very fashionable at the time. Nor is there anything to suggest why Fr Howell should choose him as architect for St Mary's.

It was S Gambier Parry who first introduced classicism to St Mary's, though a rather Elizabethanised classicism. This was the reredos that replaced Withers' gothic design. There is a photograph of this in the Clergy House (plate 4) which shows a large classical arch in a dark wood, probably mahogany, tricked out with Elizabethan details, including strapwork, cresting and a sunburst with IHS (see note 1 for details of further work on Parry's design by Martin Travers and HS Goodhart-Rendel).

Rather more important than the reredos are the organ case and loft designed by Parry around 1908 and 1913, when the original Walker organ was rebuilt by Willis and placed in the new organ case (plate 5). This is a magnificent example of Wren baroque revival with splendid Grinling Gibbonsesque carving, in a dark mahogany which greatly enhances the west end of the church and gives it the quality of a grand house that Canon Brindley talks of. This is particularly so of the panelling at the ground floor which wraps itself around the west end of Withers' church and continues under the organ gallery which is supported by a pair of perfectly proportioned square Doric columns with finely carved brackets. It is this type of hardly noticed care in small details that makes St Mary's such an important place. If, as may have to happen at some time, the choir gallery has to be enlarged it is vitally important that this Wrennian, baroque quality is carried into the new work.

## Martin Travers (1886–1948)

But it was with the arrival of the very wealthy Humphrey Whitby that St Mary's was transformed. He became vicar in 1916 at the height of the Great War and died in 1948, the year after he retired. Whitby it was who turned from Gambier Parry to the more flamboyant Martin Travers, who was not an architect but an exquisite draftsman and stained-glass artist. Travers, in 1911, was working with George Sedding, the son of the great JD Sedding of Holy Trinity, Sloane Street, when he met Humphrey Whitby, then a curate at St Columba's, Haggerston. He was commissioned to design Fr Whitby's first mass set at the time of his ordination. This is the same magnificent red set that is one of the treasures of St Mary's and one of the finest examples of twentieth-century ecclesiastical art, with its gilded Pentecostal flames contrasting with the deep scarlet silk of the vestments. While the name of St Mary's will always be linked to Martin Travers and his golden baroque design, in fact there is very little that he did here. But what he did is very important and the baroque High Altar and reredos will always have a major influence on the character of the church.

I quote from Rodney Warrener's article "Martin Travers at Bourne Street", in the Autumn 1998 issue of *Salve*. He gives the background to the churchmanship that inspired Travers and the priests of St Mary's: "To understand how Travers became so closely linked with St Mary's it is necessary to understand the viewpoint held by a certain minority of Catholic clergy and ordinands in the Church of England at the turn of the century. The second generation of Ritualists had by and large won the day with regard to Catholic ceremonial in the Anglican Church...

"At this time the liturgy in many Anglo-Catholic churches was somewhat esoteric and all types of peculiar local usage had crept in. Unnecessary adornments to shrines and altars could be seen together with choir and servers wearing virtually anything of any liturgical colour that took the incumbent's fancy... If the Catholic cause was to be taken seriously and the Church of England's part in the Western Patriarchate understood, her liturgy had to conform with that of the Roman Catholic Church in Europe and elsewhere and her teachings had to be in tune with it as far as possible. The so-called Sarum or English Use, 'British Museum Religion', was based on a supposition of what might have been prior to the 1549 Prayer Book. Constant references to a 16th-century ornaments rubric was somewhat futile by the early years of the century.

"One priest who certainly held this point of view was Fr Maurice Child [later a curate at St Mary's] who in 1910, whilst still a curate at St Andrew's, Haverstock Hill, brought together a group of priests and some influential members of the laity to found the Society of St Peter and St Paul. It started in the Medici Society who had produced Lord Halifax's *Mass Book of Edward VI*. By the following year it was a properly constituted society and Mr Samuel Gurney was its unpaid secretary. Amongst its original founders were Ronald and Wilfred Knox, the Duke of Argyll, Cyril Howell and NP Williams (Chaplain of Exeter College, Oxford). Most of the clergy were associated with St Mary's Graham Street, as it was then known. Fr Howell being its vicar and Wilfred and Ronald Knox assistant associate priests...

"The ideals of SSPP were to further ultramontane Anglo-Catholicism as far as it was possible and their publications were produced in 17th- and 18th-century format depicting devotions of the Latin Rite often adapted for Anglican use with the 1662 Prayer Book" (op cit pp 20-21).

The Society of St Peter and St Paul published two volumes on the Mass entitled *Pictures of the English Liturgy: Vol I High Mass* (1916) and *Vol II Low Mass* (1922) designed to show how it should be done in the 'correct' Tridentine manner and Martin Travers illustrated these elegant volumes. The Low Mass set shows the priest celebrating Mass at a baroque altar, but the High Mass volume gets more exotic in each drawing. As Travers moves through the Mass he displays a different style of altar, Baroque or Rococo, in each plate. It is almost as if he is offering Fr Whitby alternatives for St Mary's altar. The sarcophagus altar depicted in the censing of the altar at the introit (plate 6) is very similar to that chosen for St Mary's.

In 1916 Fr Whitby had the chance to put these ideals into practice. Martin Travers was asked to adapt the high altar and reredos at St Mary's. He produced a sarcophagus-shaped altar in gilded wood with an accompanying gradine, tabernacle and six baroque candle sticks. The existing reredos by Gambier Parry remained. Five years later it was decided to erect a memorial to Fr Cyril Howell and Travers designed the basic reredos that is in St Mary's today (plate 7). It was intended to have rood figures of our Lady and St John on either side but these never materialised.[1] Other pieces in the church dating from this period include six large hearse lights and a ciborium cover embroidered with the emblem of the Sacred Heart surrounded by thorns surmounted with a crown and flames. The statue of our Lady of Peace was designed in 1920[2] (plate 9) and originally stood in the north aisle prior to the alterations of the 1930s.

The walnut sedilia by Travers was made in 1922. His ornate high altar (Easter) frontal dates from 1924.

"Travers did prepare drawings for the enlargement of St Mary's in the 1920s[3] showing the Chapel of the Seven Sorrows containing the existing statue of our Lady of Peace, a confessional box, and plain arched windows in the north wall. The officers of the parish [the Trustees?] decided not to entrust this development to him and instead chose HS Goodhart-Rendel. We are told that Travers was extremely hurt at this decision and 'walked out in a huff'. It can be said with hindsight that the decision taken was a wise one, because although Martin Travers excelled in the medium of stained glass and church furnishings, he was not experienced in building construction" (op cit p 23). It was Goodhart-Rendel who was to have most influence on the design of St Mary's as we know it today.

## HS Goodhart-Rendel (1887–1959)

Although HS Goodhart-Rendel was only a year younger he was in many ways very different from Martin Travers. He was aristocratic, inheriting Hatchlands in Surrey in 1931 from his uncle Lord Rendel, which he lived in most of his life but finally gave to the National Trust, whereas Travers was bohemian middle-class. More important, Goodhart-Rendel was a fine architect but Travers merely a ravishing decorator. Goodhart-Rendel fought in the Brigade of Guards in both wars, whereas Travers went to neither war although he was in the Red Cross. Probably most important of all, Goodhart-Rendel was a practising Catholic, who became a Roman Catholic in 1936, whereas Travers seems to have had no faith whatsoever! But both Travers and Goodhart-Rendel, and indeed in a less marked way Gambier Parry, all had an understanding of past styles which at the time were unfashionable and approached their job not in an arid historicist manner but with wit and style. It is this wit mixed with high art that makes the interior of St Mary's so special.

Goodhart-Rendel, who became President of the RIBA in 1938, began his distinguished career both as architect and architectural historian in 1904 by designing cottages and lodges for his family and friends. Up until 1914 he had done little work of importance except for one large house in Englefield Green and The Eton Boys' Club in Hackney Wick. After the Great War, when he was wounded, he had still done little of note by 1922 when he was first commissioned to work at St Mary's. He began not in the church, where Martin Travers still held sway, but by converting a pub called "The Pineapple" on the corner of Graham Terrace and Bourne Street, into a presbytery.

This he did with great style replanning it, adding another floor in a mansard roof, at the quite high cost (in 1922) of £8,300. Outside nothing of the pub is now visible. The ground floor pub windows have been replaced with brickwork and the whole of the rest is hung with blue slates with a sharply pitched roof formed over the old flat roof of the pub. In the gable is a completely original Gothic-Venetian window. The building was designed as, and is still used as, a number of flats for the clergy, with a dining room and library on the first floor. Here Goodhart-Rendel allowed the fine Victorian deep skirtings, fireplaces and cornices to remain. Lit with his tall casement windows these fine rooms combine the best of Victorian and fashionable 1920s architecture, and give us a foretaste of what he was to achieve within the church.

As we have seen, when it was decided to extend the church in the early 1920s, Fr Whitby turned from the baroque extravagance of Travers to Goodhart-Rendel who at the time was just discovering High Victorian gothic well before his contemporaries or the bright young things of the next generation such as John Betjeman and Kenneth Clarke. Clarke's *The Gothic Revival—an Essay in the History of Taste* is much praised as the first serious attempt to look at the Victorian gothic revival though in fact his views are still tinged with rather unthinking Victoriana. It was not published until 1929, when Goodhart-Rendel was completing his Gothic re-revival work at St Mary's.

Originally Withers' church was entered through Graham Terrace but when it became necessary to enlarge St Mary's a new entrance was made in Bourne (then Westbourne) Street by taking down a house. The house between this and the new presbytery was also bought and was altered by Goodhart-Rendel. In 1972 it was to become the nuns' home, complete with chapel on the first floor (Appendix III).

The courtyard formed is quite sharply angled from the church, but Rendel has cleverly disguised this by designing a red brick entrance porch with a delightful octagonal tower which houses the Choir Room over it in very much the manner of the late Victorian gothic revival architects such as JL Pearson. The side walls to the houses are diapered brickwork, also in a Victorian manner. On entering we find that the splendidly vaulted porch is not an octagon but rather an irregular seven-sided room which, were it regular, would be a nonagon. As you enter through the wide door the opening seems to repeat directly in front, leading to the new north aisle of the church. It is only by looking carefully that it becomes obvious that this is in fact not a direct entrance for, far from being a regular octagonal porch, there are in fact three sides to the left and only two to the right. Goodhart-Rendel has rather subtly turned the visitor some thirty degrees to the left and brought them into line with the main church without their being aware of it. This is clearly seen by looking at Goodhart-Rendel's floor decoration in the porch which shows a star with nine points each separated from the next by 40 degrees.

From the porch we enter a passage. At the end are doors which lead into a kind of flat-ceilinged narthex, with clerestory windows to one side. To the right is the beginning of an arcade, which contains a dark but baroque reredos without an altar, by Goodhart-Rendel, who it would seem was not adverse to designing in the baroque manner if his clients wished it. Tucked in behind the doors is a small vaulted area that Goodhart-Rendel calls on his plan a "Crib". This is the site of the new Columbarium. High up above is a painting of St Christopher by Anne Walke. Beyond the narthex, we enter Goodhart-Rendel's new north aisle, called the Seven Sorrows' chapel.

This whole aisle is a remarkable case of 'keeping in' with the Withers church. It is almost impossible to appreciate how little-liked

Victorian architecture was in the 1920s. Following Lytton Strachey all things Victorian were laughed at but Victorian architecture came in for particular derision and was almost universally considered hideous. The Victorian Society was only founded 35 years later, in 1958, by Goodhart-Rendel amongst others, and even then they had a hard battle to convince the public that as fine a building as Scott's St Pancras Hotel was worth preserving. In the 1920s it was considered by everyone, including Martin Travers, that the only way to treat a Victorian polychrome interior was to paint it white.

Goodhart-Rendel has something to say about this in his essay in the St Mary's *Quarterly* of 1925: "Many coloured bricks are not frequently seen nowadays, the fashion of the moment is for white-wash, and from many people it is useless to expect more than toleration even for the noble brick-lined churches of Brooks and of Pearson." At that time Goodhart-Rendel was the only architect who could have written such a sentence, even the great Ninian Comper was a whitewasher. Travers whitewashed the whole of the interior of Butterfield's magnificent St Augustine's, Queen's Gate, so as to show off his great gilded reredos there, five years after Goodhart-Rendel wrote his defence of red brick. It is extremely fortunate that Travers was not allowed to get his hands on St Mary's. St Augustine's has recently had its whitewash stripped at considerable expense to reveal Butterfield's wonderful decorated brickwork.

Withers' brickwork at St Mary's is of course not of the quality of Butterfield's, and he has used rather a hard machine-made red brick, as would befit a small, poor Victorian church. Goodhart-Rendel was too much of an arts and crafts man to use this brick, and the new St Mary's was far from being a poor church, so he chose a much finer hand-made red brick and used wide mortar pointing, which gives a softer quality to his extension helped by the fact that instead of Withers' rather poor stone columns, the columns in his extension are of very fine granite.

Goodhart-Rendel was presented with a tricky problem, both in marrying his better materials to Withers' church but also in extending Withers' narrow north aisle in a way that does not jar.

---

He has pulled this off quite brilliantly. He wrote of the desirability of not doing away with Withers' aisle, his half arches, and of the need to adjust the architectural character between the new and old "without discord but without anachronisms." It is difficult to see what he meant by that since his design positively delights in anachronism.

In the place of Withers' north wall Goodhart-Rendel has built an arcade of arches, which reflect Withers' arches but spring at a lower level (plate 10), which when seen from the main body of the church suggests, by false perspective, a wider aisle. This arcade is particularly successful where it frames the statue of our Lady of Peace. The granite columns themselves rise to the arches without any capitals with mouldings in granite then in brick dying smoothly into the brick arches, in contrast to Withers' rather stiff gothic capitals. This is an entirely satisfactory solution but is also a witty reference to James Brooks (the inspirer of Withers' church) since Brooks' unfinished All Hallows, Gospel Oak, has precisely these columns, which otherwise are extremely rare in the English gothic revival.

It is not just in the structure of the extension that Goodhart-Rendel harks back to the Victorians but in the design of his remarkable neo-Victorian, gothic re-revival furnishings, which are the most fascinating of all St Mary's treasures since they are unique. Gothic re-revival is rare enough today but in the 1920s, with its loathing of all things Victorian, it was quite unheard of. Yet no one at the time seems to have remarked on this fact, nor do we have any idea of what Fr Whitby or any of the other sophisticated associated priests of that time thought of these remarkable artefacts.

First, there is the magnificent reredos to the altar of the Seven Sorrows of Our Lady (plate 11). This holds a group of fine pictures by Colin Gill, signed and dated 1929, cousin of Eric Gill and a well known mural painter of the time. Rectangular, it depicts six of the Seven Sorrows in two lines, the final broad panel below, under a sweeping arch above the altar, depicts the deposition of our Lord from the cross, the final sorrow: a simple layout made remarkable by the decorations of the frame. The columns that divide the pictures are painted with lozenges and zig-zags, and the frame itself has painted blank arches rising to miniature battlements with tourelles, much in the manner of William Burges or William Morris. But instead of Burges' strong reds and golds the dominating colours here are (the then extremely fashionable) blue and silver. Below, as the reredos proper, is a carved panel in a complex design of interlocked crosses which also form swastikas (an ancient symbol of the sun, taken from Egyptian Coptic Christian designs and here covered in silver leaf). The simple stone altar is straightforwardly Victorian gothic revival.

The silver candlesticks and cross with lapis lazuli, malachite and red enamel are also extremely fine, and show just a touch of *art déco*, within the gothic revival context (plate 12). Both Goodhart-Rendel's design and working drawings are in the RIBA (dated 31.12.29, and revised 25th March 1930). They are made by the Birmingham Guild. The RIBA also has an exquisite drawing of Goodhart-Rendel's simple but complex mahogany altar rails, made up of an inter-locking pattern (plate 13). Open octagons within circles are formed with angled timber pieces, some vertical and some at thirty degrees, to form the sides of the octagons. The screen is divided by uprights with gothic-revival blank arches. This screen was made by Betty Joel, one of the most fashionable furniture makers of the period. The stained glass to the window over the altar is by Margaret Rope (1891–1988), a memorial to Fr Whitby, replacing a window blown out during the Second World War.

Perhaps even more surprising is the confessional of 1936. This piece of furniture is harsh and almost modern, yet it is in the gothic revival style. Flat roofed it has at each corner miniature gun embrasures rather than gothic tourelles, almost copies of the embrasures of the contemporary Maginot Line, but anachronistically supported on heraldically painted columns.

But probably the most remarkable piece of gothic re-revival is the domed tabernacle, with doors, to the statue of St John the Baptist in the south aisle (plate 14). The RIBA has two carefully coloured drawings of this (dated 22.11.29). This is straightforward Burges revivalism. The colouring in the RIBA drawings is even more elaborate and colourful than what was finally done. Very different is the handling of the stone base of the tabernacle. Here we find the sharp modernistic angles of Goodhart-Rendel's much praised contemporary Hays Wharf Building.

Goodhart-Rendel's talent shows at its best in the way that he is able to integrate Victorian gothic revivalism with what was at the time extreme modernism in one small item of church furnishings. The paintings of the panels are by Colin Gill, but there is no record of the designer of the statue; it may well be Martin Travers, or even J Harold Gibbins who took over some of the ideas of Goodhart-Rendel after the latter's death. Colin Gill also painted the St George and the St Edward hanging either side of the statue of St Joseph on the south aisle.

Goodhart-Rendel made a number of designs for St Mary's that were not carried out. (The RIBA has 35 of his designs and detail drawings, including the design for the extension of the vestries around the west end of the church where the large rainwater head is dated 1927 and the Carmel Hall in Bourne Street, originally the church hall and now the Grosvenor Club, which he designed in a sub-Soane style in 1937.) Of the designs not built the one most to be regretted is that for the completion of the west end of the church which was to take the place of the whole of No. 26 Graham Terrace. Inside this he created a great crossing narthex with a large choir gallery, and on the exterior a splendid tall saddle-back tower, based, he tells us, on Norman Shaw's very fine 1869 church at Lyons (plate 15).

## Post 1945

By the outbreak of war in 1939 the main works at St Mary's as we see the church today were complete. Only a few additions since then need to be noted. Goodhart-Rendel continued to work after the war (he was responsible for the buttressing on the south side of the church, needed because of bomb damage) almost up to the time of his death in 1959. His last design, which probably fortunately was never built, was for a tester over the high altar. At this point J Harold Gibbons (1878–1958), another obscure architect, the pupil of H Wilson (himself a pupil of JD Sedding) and designer of the east front of St Augustine's, Highgate, in the Wilson style, seems to have taken over since he too made a design for this, no better than Goodhart-Rendel's. It was also never built.

## Font

In 1953 J Harold Gibbons was commissioned to design the font and cover, which is built under the organ gallery. It is very much in the Goodhart-Rendel manner. The carving of the fishes around the stone base of the font have vigour, as does the carving of the wooden canopy, with a pelican in its piety at the apex. It is a fine survival of the arts and crafts tradition, which one would expect from a pupil of H Wilson, one of the great figures of the later arts and crafts movement.

## Pulpit

Originally Withers designed a stone pulpit on the north of the altar steps in the form of an ambo. This was removed in the re-ordering of the chancel and a very simple and rather temporary seeming pulpit was made using an open timber frame which was placed further down the church on the south side in the third most westerly arch. In the late 1960s it was felt by some of the grander members of the congregation that this simple and eccentrically placed pulpit could not be permitted to remain, and so a new pulpit was commissioned and paid for by George Vaizey (the Vaizey arms prominently displayed on the pulpit door). Unfortunately he turned to Laurence King (1907–81) the prolific post-war church architect for the design. King designed in a very watered down Travers style, exemplified, as Warrener remarks, in the later works of the Faith Craft Studios. The pulpit with its enormous armorial panels and its unnecessarily heavy tester, touched about in gold is too large for its position and badly detracts from both Withers' and Goodhart-Rendel's excellent work.

## Sanctuary

One further major addition has been made to the church chancel or sanctuary. In spite of all the grandeur of the High Altar, the walls beneath the arches were covered in hessian panels and painted gold and remained surprisingly tatty. A very elaborate Austrian baroque scheme had been prepared by Peter Jamieson in 1957, but this was not done. In 1974 the mahogany fielded panelling was put in. It was designed by Roderick Gradidge in a simple classical style, perhaps reflecting Canon Brindley's vision of St Mary's as a grand drawing room. It was designed as a memorial to Fr Langton. The original reordering of the chancel was a memorial to Fr Howell, Fr Whitby's predecessor, and there was a memorial plaque designed by Martin Travers recording this. This plaque was copied for an inscription to Fr Langton, and lettered by Gavin Stamp, who also painted the fine lettering to the columns on either side of the chancel.

## Bishop's Throne and Legilium

There have been two recent additions to the furnishings. First, the Bishop's Throne designed by Matthew Rice and built in the workshop of Lord Lindley in the late 1980s, and secondly the Legilium in the chapel of the Seven Sorrows, a memorial to Dr Eric Mascall, designed in 1997 by Roderick Gradidge and built by Bill Stainthorpe.

## Columbarium and Shrine of the True Cross

Finally, there are the Columbarium and its Shrine of the True Cross (Appendix IV). This is being built at the moment to designs by Roderick Gradidge, in the recess by the main entrance which Goodhart-Rendel called the Crib. It has two columns at the entrance painted (as the columns of the reredos to the Seven Sorrows altar) in chevrons, but here in black and gold. These support a frieze with biblical inscriptions in Latin relating to the theme of resurrection (*Credo videre bona domini in terra viventium*). The mahogany containers for the ashes of the faithful are fixed all round and in the centre there will be Omar Ramsden's great reliquary of the True Cross, itself in the shape of the cross with the Relic in the centre. This is fronted in glass engraved by Josephine Harris, in memory of Helena Levy. Above, in the tympana of the arches, will be three panels painted by Anthony Ballantine, representing three resurrections, first that of Christ, secondly that of the saints and martyrs and thirdly the eschatological resurrection of the body at the Last Judgement. Above, the blue vaulted ceiling will be powdered in stars by Christopher Boulter. It is interesting that this is the work of three past-masters of the Art Workers Guild and one past honorary secretary. This follows a St Mary's tradition, for Omar Ramsden was also a brother of the Guild, as were J Harold Gibbons, Colin Gill, HS Goodhart-Rendel, Laurence King and Gavin Stamp.

It is much to be hoped that this final addition to St Mary's will be of the same quality as all the many wonderful artefacts with which this church has been so plentifully endowed during the last century and a quarter. It has indeed become, as Canon Brindley put it, a place of "infinite riches in a little room."

Notes

1.  The reredos was then worked on again by Goodhart-Rendel (and only completed in 1934) who in the place of the two figures, designed the great volutes that so perfectly match the Travers design. Goodhart-Rendel also replaced Parry's IHS in the upper part with a sculptural group depicting the Coronation of the Virgin in heaven (plate 8). It is not clear when the chancel was cleared of the choir stalls and the parquet floor laid, a most important part of the design of the chancel at St Mary's as we know it. Although it seems like Travers' work it is more likely to have been by Gambier Parry when he removed the choir to the gallery. The mahogany chancel rails are very similar in style to those of the choir gallery.

2.  As a war memorial. It was said to have been based on the famous medieval statue at Amiens well known to soldiers of the Great War. However, this statue is gothic, but Travers, with judicious use of gold and silver and with a great sunburst and crown, has succeeded in making the medieval statue look baroque!

3.  (Sic!) In fact, as we will see, Goodhart-Rendel started work at St Mary's in 1922 and the main building work took place in the late 1920s and the fittings were designed in 1929. It is difficult to imagine what Travers was doing designing an extension to the church which had already been built! For instance, when in 1911 Travers first met Fr Whitby, he was living with his widowed mother at 3 Priory Gardens, Bedford Park, the 'artistic' suburb, using the studio in the garden

as his workshop. At the outbreak of war he let the studio to Christine Mac Liammøir, sister of Michel. They eloped and got married in a deserted waiting room in Birmingham station. Travers did not tell his mother of this escapade, but kept his wife in the studio whilst he lived in the house. His mother only heard that they were married when, in the early 1920s, they left for a house in Black Lion Square. Presumably this was not something that would endear Travers to Fr Whitby. For further details see *Catalogue of the Drawings at the RIBA* Vol. T–Z, and *Bedford Park 1875–1975, Catalogue of the Centenary Exhibition Victorian Society* 1975 pp. 31–2.

# The Servant of the Liturgy

## Plainsong and Polyphony ~ Shane Fletcher

THE RECORD of the musical tradition at St Mary's is surprisingly sparse, until the period after the Second World War. This is almost certainly because music was always been treated as the 'servant of the liturgy' and the musical history of St Mary's was simply not written down! From copies, however, of St Mary's *District Magazine* (up to 1906), the *Parish Magazine* (from 1906 to 1916), the *Weekly Journal* (1916–18) and the *Graham Street Quarterly* (the inspiration of Fr Whitby and still going strong when Fr John Gilling became parish priest in 1971), it is possible to piece together a general picture of the musical life in St Mary's during her first 75 years.

## 1874–1949

In 1884 church life on Sunday was very full with the Holy Communion at 7am, 8am, 9.30am and 10.30am, Matins and Sermon at 11.30am, Children's Service at 3.30pm and Evensong and Sermon at 7pm. Year after year there is no reference to music at all in these early monthly magazines with the exception of occasional references to a "St Mary's Choral Society".

### S. Mary's Choral Society.

A concert will be given by the S. Mary's Choral Society on Monday, May 5th, at 8 p.m., in S. Barnabas Boys' School-room Ebury-street (by kind permission of Rev. A. Gurney), in aid of the S. Saviour's Priory House of Rest for Men at Brighton. Tickets, 2/6-, 1/-, and -/6; to be obtained at S. Paul's Mission House, Westbourne-street ; and from Mr. Bliss, 96, Westbourne-street.

### Notices.

The Bible Instruction in St. John will commence again on May 8th, at 12, beginning at Chapter vii.

There will be a meeting of District Visitors Friday, May 9th, at 12.15.

---

Ascension Day, May 22nd.
Holy Communion, 5, 6.45, 8, 9.30, 10.30 a.m.
Matins and Sermon, 11.30.
Evensong and Sermon, 8.30 p.m.
Offertories for the Church in East London.

When the Choral Society met, with what voices, what its repertoire was—all this is unknown. It is difficult to believe it did not sing in church at all, but we have no record.

By 1909 there is still no mention of a choir in spite of full lists of a wide range of organisations including the Guild of St Joseph for men, the Band of Hope for boys, a Maternity Society and a Sewing Class for girls. Yet, Sunday services include a 'Choral' Communion and the July Patronal Festival had a lot of music, more in terms of the number of services than we have today.

## THE PATRONAL FESTIVAL

SERVICES AND PREACHERS

*Thursday, July 1st.*
Evening Prayer, solemnly sung, and Sermon
BY
REV. J. C. HOWELL,
8.30 p.m.

*Friday, July 2nd. Feast of the Visitation of the Blessed Virgin Mary.*
Holy Communion, 6.45 and 8 a.m.
Procession, Holy Communion (solemnly sung),
with Sermon, 11 a.m.
Preacher,
REV. B. S. HACK,
Vicar of St. Thomas's, Oxford.
*Sunday, in Octave, July 4th.*
Holy Communion, 7 and 8 a.m.
Morning Prayer, 10.30 a.m.
Procession, Holy Communion (solemnly sung),
with Sermon by
REV. H. F. B. MACKAY,
Vicar of All Saints', Margaret Street,
11 a.m.
Children's Service, 3 p.m.

Evening Prayer (solemnly sung), followed by
Sermon by
REV. R. E. GIRAUD,
Vicar of St. Mary Magdalene's, Munster Square,
and Procession, 7 p.m.

With the arrival of Fr Whitby we begin to see music playing a greater part in the life and worship of St Mary's, along with new societies: the Confraternity of the Blessed Sacrament, the League of the Bona Mors and the 23rd Westminster Troop of Scouts. The first *Quarterly* contained these words from Fr Whitby: "It is generally admitted that the average Parish Magazine is unsatisfactory from a religious point of view, and the result has been that many of the important Churches in London have been led to produce a magazine which is entirely their own. We feel that the time has come when St Mary's should take its place as one of this group of Churches." As well as celebrating St Mary's importance with a sermon by Fr Stanton and article on the Rosary and Confession, Fr Whitby also included lists of hymns and these Notes on the Mass.

## NOTES ON THE MASS.

The following Anthems are said or sung :

The Asperges (Psalm 51), on Sunday, at 11. a.m.

1. After the beginning of the Service. *The Introit.*

2. After the Epistle. *The Gradual.* (With *Tract, Verse, Alleluia,* or *Sequence* as appointed.)

3. After the Creed or Sermon. The *Offertory-verse.*
   [After which, at the sung Mass, a hymn or short Motet may be sung, as also after the Elevation.]

4. After the Communion of the Priest and People. *The Communion-verse.*
   A proper set of these Anthems is appointed for every Sunday and Holy Day throughout the year. They will be found at the back of the hymn-book, numbered from Advent Sunday onwards.

---

5. After the Lord's Prayer :
℣     The peace of the Lord be always with you.
℟     And with thy spirit.
     O Lamb of God, that takest away the sins of
the world, have mercy upon us, (twice)
     O Lamb of God, that takest away the sins of
the world, Grant us thy peace.

6. Before the Blessing is said or sung :
℣     Depart in peace (or, Let us bless the Lord).
℟     Thanks be to God.

The serious musical tradition of St Mary's had begun, interestingly enough, with music for the Proper of the mass, not the Ordinary.

During the inter-war period, music at St Mary's slowly established itself as an integral part not only of its liturgy but of its life. There was one unique feature of the former which was the so-called 'Hangover Mass' (at 12.15pm every Sunday) when gentle music (Brahms' Adagio from the D minor Sonata and *Berceuse* by Fauré were popular numbers) was played on the violin to a suitably subdued organ accompaniment. At the same time Fr Whitby included in the Parochial Fund a special item 'Music and Choir'. For the last quarter of 1932 the Receipts for this were £37.11.6d and the Expenditure £97.12.0d. (The total cost of four priests' stipends was only £141.4.6d! St Mary's has for a long time valued its music and been prepared to spend on it.)

The music was further enriched by the composer Anthony Bernard who with Charles A Claye wrote the *Joyous Pageant of the Holy Nativity* and the *Merry Masque of Our Lady in London Town*. The Pageant was performed at the Chelsea Palace Theatre on the King's Road, opposite the Town Hall for over forty years.

Throughout the whole of Fr Whitby's years at St Mary's music in church was in the hands of George Underwood (from 1903 to 1949). It was under him that the tradition of St Mary's of 'plainsong and polyphony' was established. Following the work of RR Terry at Westminster Cathedral from 1901 to 1924, 16th- and 17th-century polyphonic masses were sung at a time when the repetoire was barely known to the general music lover. But, at Bourne Street, they were always sung in English. Those not published in English had sticky strips of paper with the English words covering up the Latin. The Viennese masses of Haydn, Mozart and Schubert were not sung: Bourne Street 'did' polyphony and Margaret Street 'did' Viennese.

As early as 1928 Underwood was providing music for Holy Week which is reminiscent of what we do now:

## HOLY WEEK AND EASTER MUSIC.
### Palm Sunday
At the Blessing of Palms and Procession :
"Hosanna Filio David" *Casali.*
"In Monte Oliveti," Plainsong in *Faux Bourdon.*
"Pueri Hebræorum," (three settings), Plainsong, *Palestrina, Miller.*
At Mass :
Mass in C minor, *Charles Wood.*
Passion Music, *Vittoria.*
Motet, "O Bone Jesu," *Palestrina.*
### Good Friday
Passion Music, *Vittoria.*
Reproaches, *Vittoria.*
"Crux Fidelis," *John of Portugal.*
"Adoramus te Christi," *di Lasso.*
"Vexilla Regis," *R. R. Terry.*
### Holy Saturday.
Mass, Plainsong.
Organ Voluntary, Allegro, *Handel.*
### Easter Day.
Mass :
Aeterna Christi Munera, *Palestrina.*
Evening Service :
This is the Day, *Miller.*
Magnificat, *Vittoria.*
Te Deum.

Underwood also ran a very successful boys' choir which won numerous competitions for folk song and sight reading competitions; winners' certificates in 1928 and 1930, signed by Herbert Howells and Martin Shaw, are still on display in the Choir Room.

Underwood's departure coincided with the arrival of the new

parish priest, Fr Stephen Langton, who promptly appointed Underwood's assistant organist, Bob Strong. Previously, the music at High Mass had simply 'happened', but within a week it was properly advertised, a tradition which has been maintained since.

### MUSIC FOR DECEMBER.

| | |
|---|---|
| ADVENT II. | Mass, Russian ; Motet, "Liebster Jesu," *Bach.* |
| ADVENT III. | Mass, *Missa Seraphica* ; Motet, "Father of All," *Tye.* |
| ADVENT III | Mass, *Gibbons* ; Motet, "And now, O Father," *Gibbons.* |
| CHRISTMAS | Midnight Mass, Plainsong (*De Angelis*). |
| CHRISTMAS | Day Mass, Viadan (*L'Hora Passa*) ; Motet, "Love came Down," *Darke.* |

With Strong's appointment the modern period in the history of the Musical Tradition at St Mary's commences.

# 1949–99

Since 1949 St Mary's has had four parish priests, but only three organists. Conrad Lewis replaced Strong in 1968. Some ten years later this writer was appointed, having had the advantage of about three years apprenticeship in the choir as a singer.

In its closing years, Conrad Lewis' tenure was distinguished by inspired improvisations combined with the loudest stage whisper imaginable. If the subdeacon failed to sing the epistle tone correctly the versicle "This is the word of the Lord" would be answered by Conrad's "…but not the tune!" Was this really inaudible beyond the gallery? Some traditions have persisted from those days. During the singing of the litany of the saints at the Easter Vigil it is still difficult for the choir to keep a straight face; "Holy Basil" is always a problem. Perhaps the inclusion of topical but invented saints at the rehearsal beforehand does not help. At the height of a food poisoning scare, it was even suggested that there might well have been two early Roman martyrs SS Listeria and Salmonella.

By the late 1960s the general listening public caught up with St Mary's and there was widespread interest in 'early music'. Recordings were made of the very masses sung at Bourne Street—but in Latin.

---

First the three Byrd masses and a handful of those by Palestrina became available; then new groups, such as the Tallis Scholars, explored lesser known avenues of 16th-century music. It therefore seemed sensible to sing the setting of the mass, the ordinary, in the language originally conceived by the composer.

The pace of change towards a greater variety of mass settings has varied. A trickle of Viennese masses (three or four by Mozart and one by Haydn, the 'little organ mass') was greatly accelerated by the decision to include all the Mozart masses in 1991, the bicentenary of Mozart's death. All of these were performed with instrumental accompaniment. This is not as difficult a task as it may seem, since most of them only require two violins and continuo. There were some real discoveries here, and we even managed to include the grandest settings. The Requiem, for instance, was the first of several liturgical performances with orchestra on All Souls' Day. More recently and more gradually, masses with organ accompaniment have been introduced. Eclecticism rules and composers have included Puccini (the *Messa di Gloria* without the Gloria—and so known by the choir as the *Messa di*), Rossini (a reduced version of the *Petite Messe Solennelle*) and Britten. At the same time the range of masses now includes earlier works than the high Renaissance settings that so long formed the mainstay of St Mary's. The heritage of the fully polyphonic days is still maintained in the important principle that there are grand, celebratory Renaissance settings just as there are penitential Viennese ones; it is depressing to read music lists where polyphony is reserved for Advent and Lent and the major feasts are always celebrated with Viennese settings.

While the ordinary of the mass is generally now in Latin, English is used for the plainsong propers. Although not set in stone, this seems reasonable. After all, the proper changes from week to week so that intelligibility is more important; everyone knows the texts of the Kyrie, Gloria, Sanctus and Agnus. In Conrad Lewis' time the more elaborate versions of the chant were introduced with their particularly complex settings of the gradual verse. This chant is sung from the edition lovingly type set by the sisters at Wantage, and no longer available. (It would be interesting to know how many other churches sing these English versions of the chant.)

Since 1978, there have been two positions at the church; the Director of Music has been assisted by an organist. Before this date, many people had helped out at the church, of whom the most distinguished was Roger Pugh, but the first official holder of the new post was Michael Bowden, who left to be assistant at All Saints, Margaret Street, in 1987. He was succeeded by Philip Berg, now in charge of the music at the Savoy Chapel and then by James Thomas who left London last year to be Director of Music at Christ's College Brecon. The latest organist is William Whitehead, previously assistant organist at Rochester Cathedral.

The original organ of 1874 was at the east end of the south aisle. It was a two manual instrument made by JW Walker & Sons with room for many stops which were added in the closing years of the last century. In 1913 the organ moved to its present position, and the splendid screen, by Sidney Gambier Parry (half brother of Hubert Parry, the composer), was installed. Was the Flemish look of this screen inspired by Lord Halifax's Belgian connections? At this stage the organ was rebuilt by the excellent firm of Lewis; they added the third manual and its stops and improved the tonal balance of the rest of the organ. It was in 1928 that the organ took on its present form; Henry Willis and Sons rebuilt the instrument, following the building of the Seven Sorrows Chapel and the choir room. They left stop knobs for a 'chancel' division of the organ with pipes to be placed at the east end of the church. The stop knobs with their evocative names (not just a 'Flute Amabile' but a 'Corno d'Amour' as well) remain; the work was never done. Willis' enthusiasm was doubtless encouraged by the installation of the latest 'electro-pneumatic' technology that allowed pipes to stand at a distance from the organ console.

In 1982 the organ underwent a full cleaning and restoration; the work was done by N Mander. It had become unreliable and leaky. Much of the action needed complete renewal, but a decision was made largely to restore the instrument to its 1928 state, with all the

fascination of the splendid workmanship of that generation—
including miniature kid bellows to make the stops come out. At the
same time the opportunity was taken to improve the appearance of
the instrument; unsightly anglepoise-style lamps had been screwed to
the front of the case and these were removed. On July 11th, 1982,
Gillian Weir re-opened the organ with a recital including César
Franck's first *Chorale*, and a memorable account of the Duruflé
*Toccata*.

The singing of the High Mass remains the main function of the
musical establishment of St Mary's; rare among London churches,
its choir sings all year round with no summer break. ("Like the
Windmill Theatre," one priest was heard to remark, "we never
close"). This has not prevented musical activities from broadening
somewhat. Said Evensong on Sundays has now been replaced by
Sung Evensong (albeit without choir) so that the Magnificat
antiphons (some of the finest of all chant settings) can be heard. In
the late 1980s the church held music festivals in the autumn,
featuring special music at the High Mass, a series of concerts and
Baroque operas staged at the church: Purcell's *Dido and Aeneas*
and John Blow's *Venus and Adonis*. The choir has produced two
recordings, one in the 1980s made in the church with the distinctive
rumble of the District and Circle Line beneath. In 1992, the choir
moved to St Silas the Martyr, Kentish Town, to record two masses
that are not well known but which, it was felt, deserved a wider
hearing: Haydn's *Missa Brevis in F*, featuring two soprano soloists,
and Palestrina's *Missa Sanctorum meritis*. These mass settings were
interspersed with the chant for Ascension Day and for Pentecost.
Motets were also recorded, including our own edition of *Love divine
all loves excelling* in which Wesley's words are reunited with the tune
for which they were intended, Purcell's *Fairest isle, all isles excelling*.

When I first came to St Mary's I was delighted by the extent to
which the congregation joined in their music, not just the hymns,
but also the plainsong. (I was surprised recently that some of them
did not realise that they sang three different settings of the Creed.)
This confident singing is best heard at processions where hymns such

as Louis Jordan's *Though the Streets of Heaven*[1] is a firm favourite. This aspect of St Mary's musical tradition is just as vital a part of the music as the choral intricacies of a Palestrina Benedictus. And I am as struck now as I was 20 years ago by the appropriateness of the congregation continuing to pray aloud during the singing of the Agnus Dei. After all, it is not the music that is worshipped at St Mary's; but it is, we hope, music that worships.

1.  See Appendix I.

# Proclaiming the Good News

*St Mary's publishing tradition ~ Brian O'Brien*

T HE INITIALS SSPP properly belong to a long defunct society, The Society of Saints Peter and Paul. This was a non-charitable unincorporated body founded in or about 1910 by a group of friends including Fr Maurice Child (who some years later became our assistant priest at St Mary's, under Fr Humphrey Whitby). The Society was, however, principally funded by Samuel Gurney, a member of a well-known family in East Anglia; and he became the owner of most of the shares in the private limited company when the Society was incorporated in 1919. The Society's business which was carried out from premises in Hanover Square, is described in the memorandum of incorporation as being that of "Wholesale and Retail Publishers, Church Furnishers and Decorators."

That Society is perhaps best remembered for its publication of a series of Tracts: a collection of which is in the library at St Mary's. It was also a patron of Martin Travers, and it is not altogether fanciful to suppose that it was through Fr Child that Fr Whitby became acquainted with Travers: with consequences with which the congregation at St Mary's is very familiar.

In 1930 the company was voluntarily wound up, and the Society formally ceased to exist. This cannot have been caused by a crisis in Anglo-Catholicism—it was, after all, the period of the very successful Anglo-Catholic Congresses. But the Society's business had evidently become unviable, probably because the specialised market for its products (other than publications) had been largely satisfied. On the winding up, the Society's outstanding liabilities were taken over by the Church Union's publishing arm the Church Literature Association (the CLA), which accordingly became entitled to the Society's goodwill, copyrights and the right to the name.

So much by way of background, because (as is obvious) the Child/Gurney Society is not the SSPP as we know it today.

---

In or about 1938 Fr Whitby conceived the notion of publishing an Anglican Missal, as a personal venture. He was, however, advised to establish a charitable trust to own the work. Accordingly, on 2nd July 1940, a trust known as The Society of St Peter and St Paul Charitable Trust came into being. The name clearly reflects Fr Whitby's respect for the work of the former SSPP; but the minor change in the name recognised CLA's ownership of the old name.

The objects of Fr Whitby's trust—the present SSPP—are "the advancement of the Christian Religion in connection with the Church of England and the undertaking or assistance of any charitable work or activities for that purpose including in particular the preparation, writing, editing, production, publication and distributing of religious books." The Anglican Missal was published in 1941; it was in use at St Mary's for some 30 years. Those with access to a copy may notice that its publication is ascribed to The Society of SS Peter and Paul; it is understood that Fr Whitby negotiated with the CLA for the use of the old name.

The terms of the 1940 deed are unsurprisingly like those of St Mary's Trust (1923), giving wide powers (within the stated objects) to the trustees. The first trustees were Fr Whitby himself, Sir Anthony Bevir (Ecclesiastical Patronage Secretary to successive Prime Ministers) and Sir Griffith Williams.

So far as is known, the Missal was the only work ever actually published by the Trust itself. There have, however, been some later publications bearing the name (for example *All Generations Shall Call Me Blessed*, I think). This came about in this way. In the late 1950s there appears to have been established at Faith House an executive committee called the 'SSPP Committee'. It comprised at one time or another such well known Church Union/CLA names as Fr Ross (Margaret Street), Harold Riley, Percy Coleman, Gerard Irvine and Brian Brindley. The constitutionality of this committee is obscure; but it plainly purported to act under Fr Whitby's trust (and not by virtue of CLA's rights). Furthermore it is clear that the trustees (in practice, by the late 1950s at least, Sir Griffith Williams alone) allowed the committee full use of the trust income. It is understood

25.
Canon D Nicholson, parish priest 1964–1971.

26.
Fr John Gilling, parish priest 1971–1990.

27.

Tableau from *The Joyous Pageant of the Holy Nativity* created in the 1920s.

28.

A group of St Marys' scouts on their annual outing to Luxembourg in 1939.

29.
HM Queen Elizabeth and HRH Princess Margaret attending a
performance of *The Joyous Pageant of the Holy Nativity* at
Chelsea Palace Theatre in 1947.

30.
One of St Mary's
Sisters of Charity in
Caroline Terrace
about 1960. From a
painting by Charles
McCall ROI NEAC.

31.
Fr Michael Shier, curate,
Fr John Gilling, parish priest
and Canon Eric Mascall OGS
in 1974.

32.
July procession 1984.

33.
St Mary's pilgrims in Walsingham procession 1985.

34.
May procession 1996.

35.
A Nuptial Mass at
St Mary's 1997.

36.
The present parish priest Fr Bill Scott (right) and his assistant, Fr Nick Mercer.

37.
St Mary's servers out to Sunday luncheon 1999.

that the 'SSPP Committee' voted itself out of existence because it was not practical to distinguish SSPP from CLA business. The SSPP publications to which I have referred were in truth published by CLA (on behalf of SSPP).

Following Sir Griffith's death in 1974 the trustees terminated the arrangements concerning the trust income (by then, going straight to the CLA). The Church Union still undertakes the task of recovering the tax credits on the investment income, and the trustees allow it to retain the tax repayment as a fee for this and for being prepared to produce accounts.

During the last quarter-century the trustees have seen themselves as a grant-giving body, and have assisted the production of several religious works. We have also helped to restore books in the faculty library at Pusey House. And the Trust has guaranteed all St Mary's own publications (a guarantee on which there has never, to date, been a call).

In order to demonstrate the continuing connections between Fr Whitby's SSPP and St Mary's it is only necessary to name the current trustees: Canon Nicholson, Fr Scott, Mark Watson and myself.

# Catholic Privileges

*Ritual and Rite ~ Fr Stephen Young*

"WHY, EVERYONE thinks you have the whole Mass from the Latin Missal," remarked an unwary priest to Fr Whitby. He was curtly assured that the liturgy at St Mary's was "composed entirely of forms to be found in the Book of Common Prayer". "Everyone" might have been forgiven for the mistake, since music, vestments and ceremonial at Bourne Street conspired to obscure the truth of Fr Whitby's statement. Yet, truth it was, for unlike many Anglo-Catholic churches in the inter-war period, the Prayer Book rite was the basis of its liturgy although perhaps not carried out in the spirit of its author. Here then was the distinctiveness of St Mary's, that the congregation heard Cranmer's phrases, but saw the splendour of the 'Western' Rite.

How this came about, is also part of the wider story of Anglican liturgy during the last 125 years. Fundamental to Bourne Street's rôle in that story are twin loyalties: to Anglican liturgy and Catholic ritual. As we shall see, this largely accounts for the distinctive tradition that continues to draw people to our altars.

During the earliest years of St Mary's church life, the worship reflected the moderate Anglo-Catholicism of its parent parish, St Paul's, Knightsbridge. St Paul's had been an early centre of the Catholic Revival in the Church of England, but by 1874 it was no longer in the forefront of the Ritualist Movement. St Paul's not only faithfully used the Book of Common Prayer, but interpreted it in a modest though definite 'catholic' direction. This was reflected at the daughter church, St Mary's, where processions, liturgical colours, use of palms on Palm Sunday and such additions to the Prayer Book calendar as St Joseph and All Souls' Day, left no visitor in doubt about its catholic loyalties.

The Holy Communion was at the centre of its worship, yet not until 1904 was the Choral Communion rescheduled to displace Mattins at the prime time, 11am. At these services the Prayer Book text of the Communion service was supplemented by the singing of the Benedictus qui venit and Agnus Dei. There was a midnight celebration at Christmas, and an orchestra at the Whitsunday Solemn Eucharist in 1897.

Many Evangelicals were alarmed by this ritualism, but compared with other London 'shrines', Bourne Street remained cautious, even timid, in its liturgical outlook. Change, however, was not long in coming and, with the creation of St Mary's as an independent parish in 1909, the worship took on a more exuberant spirit that was part of a wider confidence spreading among Catholic-minded Anglicans. These were the beginnings of the great days of Anglo-Catholicism, when Arthur Stanton preached, and Viscount Halifax was church-warden at St Mary's. The clergy ventured to use such 'extreme' language as 'the mass' or even 'Missa cantata'. Vespers of the Dead and Stations of the Cross were among the devotions that now augmented the provisions of the BCP.

The years prior to the First World War and indeed after it, were a time when many hoped to see the English Church captured by the ideals and aspirations of the Oxford Movement. This now seems over-optimistic, yet it was that confidence and vision which inspired our familiar Bourne Street tradition. Anglo-Catholics were not alone in feeling that their worship could not be contained by the letter of the Prayer Book, and there was widespread demand for revision, yet they were not united on how this was to be achieved. The more 'advanced' looked to contemporary continental Roman Catholicism, and had no time for the inevitable compromises that produced the abortive 1928 revision. 'Sarumists' sought a revival of pre-Reformation ceremonial, and were frequently teased by the 'Romanists' for being Protestants who liked dressing up! St Mary's certainly stood on the Romeward side of this breach, at least in so far as ritual was concerned, yet it took great care not to be so identified with the 'advanced' party as to lose its Anglican identity.

Fr Whitby's appointment as vicar in 1916 can best be appreciated within this context, for this period more than any other defined the

'St Mary's' tradition. From the start he made no bones about his intentions of bringing his new charge into the forefront of the Catholic Revival within the Church of England. Reservation, already practised at Bourne Street before the War, now became the focus of the full cultus of the Blessed Sacrament including Sunday evening 'Adoration', and the Roman Holy Week services. The Prayer Book calendar was supplemented with the complexities and enrichments of the Western Rite. However, this was done in a peculiarly Bourne Street manner, as is illustrated by the use of the Prayer Book title 'Conception of the Blessed Virgin Mary' for that feast, yet the Roman title 'Immaculate Conception' for the octave day! In a similar way the ancient plainsong propers of the mass were revived, but used in English and in accordance with the Prayer Book scheme of Collects and Readings. Fr Whitby's loyalty to the Established Church is clear from his restoration of the commemoration of Charles, King and Martyr, which had been dropped from the Prayer Book along with other state services (including the 'Gun Powder Plot') in the previous century.

Perhaps the most telling insight into Fr Whitby's understanding of liturgy was his solution to the vexed question of the Prayer Book Consecration Prayer. Almost all Anglo-Catholics were dissatisfied with Cranmer's idiosyncratic order of prayers at this vital point in the Mass and wished for something more definitely catholic. Many supplied the defect by silently interpolating the Roman Canon into the English service. Whitby disapproved of this as an 'annihilating' practice that obscured the integrity of both rites. Instead, he adopted the solution later known as the 'Interim Rite' (eventually this was authorised as Series I and is the basis of our present rite at High Mass), in which the prayer of oblation and 'our Father' were moved from their Cranmerian position after communion to follow the prayer of consecration. Thus, at a stroke, the catholic sequence of prayers was restored whilst retaining the Prayer Book material.

Such preoccupation with the detail of the liturgy may seem trivial from today's perspective, yet it led to the establishment of a tradition that combined the eloquence of Cranmer's prose with the splendour of Roman ceremonial. What is more, this unique blend of words and ritual has survived the upheavals of the last 30 years. No mean feat, given that the liturgical revolution of the post-war period has presented Anglo-Catholicism with some of the more perplexing challenges of its history.

The Second Vatican Council not only shook the structures of the Roman Catholic Church, but had a profound effect on Anglo-Catholics throughout the 1960s and 1970s. Having lived with the ambiguity of the rival claims of Rome and Canterbury, they were now presented with new liturgical choices. There were suddenly two sets of English rites on offer, the translation of the 'Missa Normativa' provided by Rome, and the General Synod's 'alternative services'. Many did not find this a difficult choice to make, and were soon performing the Roman option complete with fashionable minimalist ceremonial, against a backdrop of reordered churches purged of unnecessary imagery. Others made what they could of the Alternative Service Book, and brightened it up with all kinds of new and exciting ideas from the Liturgical Commission's handbook.

Amid the resulting confusion and diversity, St Mary's continued to do what it had always done! Yet, Bourne Street has never been unaffected by wider developments in liturgical worship. By retaining its Prayer Book tradition, taking what is valuable from new rites, and interpreting ceremonial change in a traditional manner, St Mary's has emerged at the end of the 20th century with a sense of continuity, transcendence and a respect for quality in worship, that seeks to lead souls to God.

# Garments of Salvation

*St Mary's vestments ~ Timothy Ashurst*

MANY learned words have been written on the origin and development of liturgical vestments and their colours. That the use of vestments was an established fact of life in England at the time of the Reformation, albeit with regional variations unique to this realm, should come as no surprise, England being a Catholic country: indeed in the presbytery library there is a substantial volume with the deceptively simple title *English Liturgical Colours*. Nor does the tale of their enforced fall into desuetude and subsequent rehabilitation need to be rehearsed here.

This is a book about St Mary's, so this is an article on the vestments at St Mary's. What do we have, and how did they get here? Neither question is as easy to answer as might be suspected, for myths grow around objects and obscure their true nature, and the absence of old inventories giving details of provenance makes the second question almost impossible to answer.

It is all too easy to talk in glib superlatives, "the finest, the largest, the most representative collection in the Church of England", or whatever other exaggeration you will. This, sadly, is simply not realistic. It is, however, true to say that the vestments belonging to St Mary's comprise the best private collection of antique vestments of any parish church in the Church of England, unrivalled in both quality and extent, including some truly outstanding examples of their type, all of which, with but one notable exception, are still in regular use.

But what is this one notable exception? Most churches, if not cathedrals, would be more than content with having one 500 year-old vestment. But St Mary's is not: there are two chasubles of about 500 years age, one of which is still used for the Feasts of St Andrew and the Exaltation of the Holy Cross, the other (perversely the younger) being too fragile for use.

It may come as a surprise to hear that the vast majority of

St Mary's 'major' vestments have been acquired during the last half century or so, following the death of the legendary Fr Whitby. It is to his bequest that St Mary's owes a beautiful, simple, violet Low Mass set, with a decidedly curious previous history, which is in perfect keeping with the Bourne Street ethos. It appears in the catalogue produced for the Festival of Vestments and Flowers, held at the church in 1979, as follows:

> 21. Chasuble, English, circa 1880. Purple silk damask. Made from a ball dress belonging to Fr Whitby's grandmother. Bequeathed by him, 1948.

There is not really very much more that can be said about that chasuble, is there?

## High Mass

Frivolity and oddity aside, the most stunning reminder of Fr Whitby in the vestments is the best red High Mass set (plate 18). As mentioned elsewhere in this book, Fr Whitby was a man of discernment and some substance. His first mass, sung at St Columba's, Haggerston in 1911, must have been an amazing sight, for this set of vestments was made for that occasion, designed for Fr Whitby by Martin Travers, when Travers was working with GE Sedding, son of JD Sedding, the architect of Holy Trinity, Sloane Street. They are of heavy red Italian silk damask. The chasuble is powdered with tongues of fire and monograms in gold thread and coloured silks. The dalmatic and tunicle are likewise embroidered with trails of naturalistic ornament and monograms with tongues of fire on the dalmatic only (representing the ordination to the diaconate), with extremely dangerous glass beaded tassels on the backs. The hood of the cope, similarly embroidered in gold thread and coloured silk, represents the descent of the Holy Spirit.

That, however is not quite the whole story. The cope has a second, plain velvet, hood. Why? To find the answer to this, we need to turn back to the Autumn edition of the St Mary's *Quarterly* in 1954, and in so doing we enter the realms of St Mary's myths and legends, for here we encounter two:

> *Most readers of the "Quarterly" know that the best red High*
> *Mass vestments are those worn by Fr Whitby at his First*
> *Mass, and given by him to St Mary's. The hood of the cope is*
> *embroidered with a picture of the descent of the Holy Ghost at*
> *Pentecost, and he had hoped that they would be used only at*
> *Whitsun, and a second set of red vestments was made for feasts*
> *occurring on Sundays. He and everyone else were extremely*
> *disappointed at the result, for with the lighting in the sanctuary,*
> *they appeared black. In consequence they have seldom been used,*
> *and the best red vestments have been used in their place.*

This comfortably explains the presence of the second, plain hood,
and ties in neatly with a legend which I encountered at the time of
producing an inventory of all the church property in 1993. There
was talk of a red velvet High Mass set lent without authority to Ely
Cathedral, and would I be going to Ely to reclaim it? No, I would
not, for it was Fr Whitby's to dispose of as he saw fit, and he saw fit
to give it away. The entry in the *Quarterly* continues:

> *A magnificent eighteenth-century Spanish rosy-red set of vest-*
> *ments has now been obtained for the church. The Trustees have*
> *advanced one hundred pounds and I am now asking the congre-*
> *gation to make up the £120. They are of the very finest brocade,*
> *interwoven with flowers and gold ornamentation, and are cut on*
> *a pattern used in Spain in the late part of the seventeenth and*
> *early eighteenth centuries. The cope is cut particularly fully, and is*
> *one of the most handsome I have ever seen.*

We continue the story in the words of Fr Langton, writing in the
Winter 1963 Quarterly:

> *A red High Mass set of woven brocade of Spanish shape and of*
> *early eighteenth-century origin came from the private chapel of a*
> *Spanish grandee, Though it is extremely heavy, its cut is so good*
> *that it is easy to wear. Unfortunately, the humeral veil is missing,*
> *for it was taken by the wife of the grandee from the private chapel*
> *sacristy to be used as a table runner. It must have been a lovely*
> *table runner, and would be a magnificent background to the very*
> *elaborate silver and glass with which the dinner table was*
> *adorned.*

Alas, Fr Langton was misinformed. If only this story were true, but it is not. This set of vestments is French, dating from about 1839. The cope does, however, redeem the situation by having apparently a will of its own: as a result of its being so extremely heavy (and, I should imagine anything but easy to wear) and stiff, it is quite possible for a priest of slender proportion to genuflect and find that the cope remains standing, teepee-like. When the rose pink High Mass set was awaiting and later undergoing restoration, this set was used in its stead, and I remember an occasion when it was used as a gold set, on the basis that it was rarely used and had so much gold in it that it might just pass for being gold anyway!

But it is not only Fr Langton who greatly admired the cut of this set of vestments. The last newly-commissioned High Mass set at St Mary's is a splendid green one, complete with lectern fall, missal and book covers and tabernacle veil. This was made towards the end of Fr Gilling's tenure at St Mary's, by David Smith, then a regular server at the altar and now a Roman Catholic priest. He too was taken by the cut of the second red set, and used it as the model for the set which the parochial church council commissioned him to make. But what we see in church today is not the original finished product. The dalmatic and tunicle were originally fitted with bows on the shoulders to match the (admittedly salmon pink) linings. Alas, the sacerdotal scissors were taken to these and gold ones put in their place!

This new green set is not the only instance of using existing vestments as models for new vestments. St Mary's most modern High Mass vestments are also green, and not at all to this writer's taste. Very unusually, however, they are equipped with apparels—separate collars for the celebrant, deacon and sub-deacon—as is another set of High Mass vestments, which is also the subject of a St Mary's myth. From the Winter *Quarterly*, 1948:

> St Mary's has many beautiful vestments, including a magnificent
> white, eighteenth-century, High Mass set, which is used only on
> the greatest festivals. There is also a magnificent cloth of gold set,
> complete with cope. This is used on the other great festivals, but

*we have never had a workday white High Mass set, and the*
*two white dalmatics which were used with a different chasuble,*
*have completely worn out. An eighteenth-century Spanish set,*
*consisting of chasuble, dalmatic and tunicle, together with remains*
*of a cope, were discovered in August, the price of which was £45.*
*The parish priest asked for the sum of £65, which would include*
*the necessary making up of the cope into stoles, maniples and*
*veils. The £43 was given, so the vestments have been bought. The*
*sum of £22 is necessary so that they can be made ready for use*
*on the Sundays after Easter.*

Actually, this set is Italian, *circa* 1870–80, in white silk reproduced from French 18th-century silk. Of this set, Fr Langton had the following to say:

*It is doubtful if there is another set of collars in use in the Church*
*of England. Their origin is similar to the apparelled albs worn in*
*the strictest Sarum churches.*

This white set is always used at Marian feasts, when it is supplemented by a fine cope which has a rather charming story behind its acquisition.

The cope has recently been restored, the original cloth of gold of the body of it having perished. The orphreys and hood are of blue velvet, the hood being embroidered with a canvas *appliqué* figure of our Lady. It is English, and dates from the early part of the 20th century. It was bequeathed to St Mary's in 1955 by WHV Tether, who had earlier given it to Fr AE Cornibeer on condition that should Fr Cornibeer predecease him, the cope was to be returned to him. He did, it was and, although Mr Tether was not a regular member of the congregation at St Mary's, he had a great devotion to the church, such that the cope was bequeathed to St Mary's on his death.

Reference was made earlier to a hybrid white High Mass set. St Mary's still has one hybrid set of High Mass vestments, a green set referred to as the Harlequin set, comprising a French pre-revolutionary chasuble of green silk shot with gold, embroidered with gold thread in neo-classical forms, and completely 'mix and match' dalmatic and tunicle made of, for the outer orphreys, French silk of *circa* 1720, for the bar orphreys, reproduction Italian silk, for the arm pieces early 20th-century silk, and topped off with very early 20th-century braid.

The Winter *Quarterly* of 1948 made reference to a magnificent white, 18th-century, High Mass set, used only at the great feasts. Made of white silk, they are Italian, and date from the first half of the 18th century. They are heavily embroidered with floral patterns in silks and gold thread. Cardinal's tassels are embroidered on each vestment, as is also a religious badge. They are reputed to have belonged to Cardinal Mendoza, but the embroidery of the badge as well as the tassels could suggest that they come from a religious house under the patronage of a cardinal. The humeral veil, while similar, is not of the set, and is said to be of Portuguese origin, but it is of inferior quality to the set as a whole. Unfortunately, it is only possible to get an indication of what they must originally have looked like from the maniples, for the whole remainder of the set has been covered with a fine protective gauze which tends to make them appear slightly pink. Proof of the scale of the work involved in producing a set of vestments like this, if proof be needed, is there if you lift the hood of the cope—there is no embroidery underneath.

Equally impressive, although in a completely different way, is the black High Mass set, a really magnificent example of the work of Louis Grosse & Co. It is truly black and truly velvet, and was made in about 1925, when black was, of course, the liturgical colour for Good Friday as well as for Requiem Masses. For this reason the number of items comprising the set is much greater than usual; in addition to the chasuble, stole and maniple for the celebrant, dalmatic, stole and maniple for the deacon and tunicle and maniple for the sub-deacon, plus cope, burse and chalice veil for Requiem Mass, there are folded chasubles for the deacon and sub-deacon, a broad stole for the deacon, and three plain deacons' stoles and maniples for the deacons of the Passion. The folded chasubles are in use for Low Mass, the stoles for the deacons of the Passion likewise: only the broad stole no longer remains intact, having been chopped up to make a lectern fall.

Apart from these sets described in detail above, there are six further High Mass sets at St Mary's. The cloth of gold set, mentioned in the 1948 *Quarterly*, is sadly beginning to show its age, owing to the fact that it is very difficult to keep cloth of gold clean where it is constantly touched. The cope, however, retains most of its original splendour.

The rose pink set has been almost completely remade; it looks fine from a distance, but close up it is only too easy to see that pieces have been replaced with similar, but not identical, silk. Somewhere along the line, St Mary's also acquired a second rose pink cope, which was technically made to be used only by a bishop, as the morse is made of enamel, set with cabochon garnets and baroque pearls—under the old rules, only bishops were permitted to wear copes with jewelled morses.

There are three violet High Mass sets. The first is a companion to the rose pink set, and was originally of the same scale as the black set (with the addition of an humeral veil); its folded chasubles and Passion deacons' stoles have met the same fate as their black counterparts. (The colour for Palm Sunday used to be violet.) The second is one of only three overtly modern High Mass sets in St Mary's, made of a vivid purple hopsack material; it lacks a cope, but has two further matching chasubles and stoles (together with burses and veils). The final violet set was given in 1984/85, made by a parishioner. It is in finely patterned velvet, and reflects the then liturgical practice at St Mary's of using a second sub-deacon to carry the Cross on other than green Sundays.

Finally, there is a white concelebration set of vestments, of Gothic shape and very free-flowing. This is used only occasionally, in years when the Maundy Thursday High Mass is concelebrated. It was given by Fr David Skeoch, a former assistant, non-stipendiary curate.

## Low Mass

With the exception of the Mendoza and Whitby sets, however, the High Mass vestments are completely eclipsed in quality by the

---

collection of Low Mass vestments, and even then there there are finer examples of embroidery than the Mendoza set in the Low Mass vestment chests. The obvious place to start an examination of the notable Low Mass vestments, is at the beginning in date terms, with the two medieval chasubles.

The (possibly) older of the two is English, late 15th or early 16th century. It is made of Italian red silk velvet, embroidered in England in the style commonly known as *opus Anglicanum*. It could have been cut down into its current shape from a full Gothic chasuble in the early 17th century, as some of the spangles date from then, the remainder being original. This vestment is still used, as stated above, on the feasts of St Andrew and the Exaltation of the Holy Cross. The other is of early 16th-century English red velvet, the orphrey being embroidered in floss silk and metal thread. Both the velvet and the orphrey have been repaired, the former by replacement of a section at the top and the latter by much overworking. Until recently it used to be brought out on the first Sunday of Advent. Owing to its condition, it is now no longer possible for this vestment to be worn. This is a pity, as it is a piece of great beauty, with the aura of history surrounding it, and it deserves to be seen, but it was a gift from a parishioner in memory of her sister, so its loan to a museum might prove problematical.

This writer has, over the course of the last few years, had the great pleasure to act as *locum* sacristan (fortunately never at Holy Week and Easter!); one of the most satisfying sights is the sacristy with the Mendoza vestments laid out on the High Mass vesting chest and three magnificent cloth of gold, silver and gold embroidered chasubles laid out ready for use in the inner sacristy. Of these three, the most unusual is an early 18th-century Portuguese chasuble, made of cloth of silver, heavily embroidered in gold thread and coral beads—surely the only chasuble one could imagine using on the feast of Our Lady of the Rosary? The second, colloquially known as the "whole armour of God" (on account of its great weight) is another bequest from Fr Whitby. It, too, is of cloth of silver, heavily embroidered in arabesque forms with gold thread. Its description in an early list of some of St Mary's vestments is as follows: "A large and heavy gold chasuble, in the florid and debased taste of the late 18th century"—a triply inaccurate description, as it is cloth of silver, *circa* 1740, and is in the best possible taste. One can recall a mass on Easter Monday being delayed, on account of the priest sinking under the weight of this chasuble while vesting and a replacement Low Mass set being arranged. The third, although every bit as heavy as the second, is not actually cloth of gold at all. It is Italian, made at Piedmont *circa* 1740, and of white silk, very heavily embroidered with gold thread and spangles.

In addition to the above best 'gold' sets, there are three best white sets, one late 19th/early 20th century and two from the third quarter of the 18th century. The latest of the three, referred to as the 'Jellybeans' on account of its rather exuberant decoration, is of white silk of Central European origin embroidered in coloured silk and cotton, incorporating earlier embroidery and decoration. It is interesting to note that silk of this period was weighted with tin, which has caused some wearing away, leaving the cotton ground exposed. The other two best white sets are of similar age, but different origin. The one is Italian, *circa* 1755–65, made of white patterned silk of French origin, embroidered in gold thread and coloured silks. This embroidery is, despite the fact that it does not stand out so brilliantly, of a finer quality than that on the Mendoza High Mass set. The other is French, from the third quarter of the 18th century, of white silk embroidered with flowers in coloured silk. Regrettably, neither of these two chasubles can be seen properly for they have both had to be covered with protective gauze which inevitably takes away much of their brilliance.

Fr Bill Scott's favourite Low Mass chasuble is definitely worthy of mention, and not just for that reason. It is possibly the most beautiful Low Mass set at St Mary's. All that survives of it are the chasuble and stole, the remaining pieces having been lost at some stage over the last three hundred years. It is of plain red silk, embroidered very heavily in thin silver gilt thread, of Portuguese origin and dating from the third quarter of the 17th century. It has been suggested that this set was made in Macao in a convent settlement. The embroidery on it is particularly elaborate, and close inspection will reveal that the Habsburg Eagle has been incorporated into the design.

The sacristy is fully equipped with Low Mass sets of every liturgical colour, including not one, but two, rose pink sets. The remainder of these, while being of good quality, are unremarkable.

It also goes without saying that St Mary's is fully equipped to deal with pontifical celebrations. There are three mitres: precious, gold and simple. The precious mitre is English, late 19th century, and at a pinch could be said almost to be similar to the Mendoza vestments, with which it does look very fine. There are gloves, tunicle and dalmatic for the use of the bishop, (although it must be said that it is easier to inveigle bishops into wearing the last item rather than the first two) as well as a fine gremial veil.

Fr Whitby's red High Mass set is not the only example of the work of Martin Travers in the sacristy. The best altar frontal, recently restored by Maureen Styler in memory of three of St Mary's servers who died in 1997, Eric Hawkins, Colin Dence and Reg Morris, was designed by him in 1924 for the High Altar and, as it was with his work that the main body of this article commenced, it seems only right to give the last word to him, with a reference to a thing of exquisite beauty which is almost never now seen. It is a ciborium cover, designed by Travers in 1919, of white silk, embroidered with the Sacred Heart, surrounded with thorns, surmounted by a crown and flames, blood drops and a glory, the whole enclosed in conventionalised volutes executed in gold thread—and that is, after all, what it is all about.

# Appendices

Mater creatoris,
Domus aurea,
Mater salvatoris,
Cæli janua:
Meet it is thy praises
Every tongue should sound
Mary over all things
To all ages crowned.

# Though the streets of Heaven

*Music by Louis Parker ~ Words by Wilfred Knox, 1921*

THOUGH the streets of Heaven,
Mary, thou dost tread,
Roses in thy bosom,
Stars about thy head;
Though before thy presence
Angels bow the knee,
Hear the supplication
Sinners make to thee.
*Mater creatoris,*
*Domus aurea,*
*Mater salvatoris,*
*Cæli janua:*
*Meet it is thy praises*
*Every tongue should sound*
*Mary over all things*
*To all ages crowned.*

In the heart of heaven
Perfect is thy rest;
Yet thou once didst wander,
Jesus on thy breast;
Poor, and scorned and helpless
Thou thy Son didst tend,
All who toil and suffer,
Mary, Maid, befriend.
*Mater creatoris...*

Though with Christ thou dwellest
Evermore at one,
Yet thou once didst seek him,

Sorrowing, thy Son;
Anxious hearts that tremble,
Heavy eyes that wake,
Into thy protection,
Mary, Mother, take.
*Mater creatoris...*

Midst the heavenly treasures
Happy though thou be,
Call to mind thy vigil
By the bitter Tree;
Mothers sorrow laden,
Widowed brides that weep,
By thy intercession,
Mary, Mother, keep.
*Mater creatoris...*

When upon our death-beds
Earthly comforts fade,
Mary, let thy presence
Keep us unafraid;
When the books are opened.
And the judgement set,
Mary, be our succour,
Pleading for us yet.
*Mater creatoris...*

# Chronological history

1874    The church, built by RJ Withers, is dedicated
to St Mary the Virgin.

1880    Sisters from St Saviour's Priory begin work at St Mary's.

1905    Death of Fr Wentworth Hankey.

1908    Death of Prebendary Villiers of St Paul's, Knightsbridge.

1909    Becomes independent parish and patronage vested
in trustees (later St Mary's Trust).
Induction of Reverend JC Howell as first parish priest.

1910    Society of SS Peter and Paul founded
by Fr Maurice Child and others.

1913    Bishop of London officiates at special mission of Lent.
Organ removed to present position in design
by S Gambier-Parry.

1916    Death of Fr JC Howell, first vicar of St Mary's.
Induction of Fr EOH Whitby by the Lord Bishop
of Kensington on the Feast of St Etheldreda.

1919    11th May, Bishop of London inaugurates
Confraternity of Our Most Holy Redeemer.

1920    29th June, first Anglo-Catholic Congress held
at Royal Albert Hall.

1921    Lord Halifax involved in Malines Conversations
in Mechelen, Belgium.

1922    Pineapple public house, 26 Graham Street
        (Bell House) and Carmel Hall acquired.

1923    St Mary's Trust re-founded.
        4th July, blessing of new presbytery, converted
        from the Pineapple public house.

1924    2nd July, St Mary's celebrates 50 years.

1925    December, *A Joyous Pageant of the Holy Nativity*, created
        by Charles Claye and Anthony Barnard, performed
        by players of St Mary's Graham Street and later
        transferred to Chelsea Palace Theatre.

1926    2nd July, first stone of the enlarged church is laid and
        blessed, where the altar of the new chapel will stand.

1928    Organ rebuilt by Henry Willis & Sons.

1930    23rd March—6th April, Solemn Mission.

1931    15th October, Fr Whitby attends the translation of the
        statue of our Lady of Walsingham to the new shrine.

1933    Centenary of the Oxford Movement. Fr Whitby
        attends service at St Mary the Virgin at Oxford.

1934    19th January, death of Lord Halifax.
        St Mary's celebrates Diamond Jubilee with appeal
        for funds to complete high altar.

1935    2nd January, memorial to Lord Halifax erected on
        west wall and unveiled by Archbishop of Canterbury.

1938    Westbourne Street re-named Bourne Street.

1939  Men drafted to war. Children evacuated to safer places.
East window (Seven Sorrows) damaged by bomb blast.

1945  Peace Day Service to commemorate end of war.

1947  10th December, HM Queen Elizabeth
and HRH Princess Margaret Rose attend *A Joyous Pageant
of the Holy Nativity* at Chelsea Palace Theatre.

1948  1st January, Fr Whitby resigns the living of St Mary's.
3rd February, induction of Revd FEPS Langton
as parish priest.
September, death of Fr Whitby.

1954  Last performance of *A Joyous Pageant
of the Holy Nativity* at Chelsea Palace Theatre.

1955  Carmel Hall sold by Trustees.

1960  Death of Charles Claye, creator of *A Joyous Pageant
of the Holy Nativity.*

1964  Fr Langton resigns through ill health.
Induction of Canon D Nicholson as parish priest.

1971  Canon Nicholson retires.
Induction of Fr John Gilling as parish priest.

1974  St Mary's Centenary.

1975  Walsingham Pilgrimage; Walsingham Festival at St Mary's.

1976  Pilgrimage to Santiago de Compostella. Bishop of London
officiates at opening of Mission to Pimlico with Canon
Gonville ffrench-Beytagh as Missioner.

---

1979    Festival of Flowers and Vestments. HRH Princess
        Margaret Rose attends Solemn Benediction
        to celebrate 70 years of St Mary's as a parish.

1982    Organ restored by NP Mander.
        Pilgrimage to Santiago de Compostella.
        'Diamond in Pimlico'. Missioner, Fr Diamond.

1983    CSP Sisters depart from St Mary's and not replaced.

1984    St Mary's inaugurated as member of Walsingham Cell.

1990    Fr John Gilling retires.

1991    Induction of Fr Bill Scott as parish priest.

1992    Ordination of women to the priesthood
        in the Anglican church.
        Audit day to review the life and work of St Mary's.

1993    Pilgrimage to Santiago de Compostella.
        Death of Canon EL Mascall.

1995    Cardinal Danneels and the Bishop of London preside
        at Solemn Evensong to celebrate the conclusion
        of Malines Conversations 70 years ago.

1998    St Mary's and St Barnabas amalgamate.

1999    St Mary's celebrates 125 years, and 90 years as a parish.
        New Columbarium unveiled.

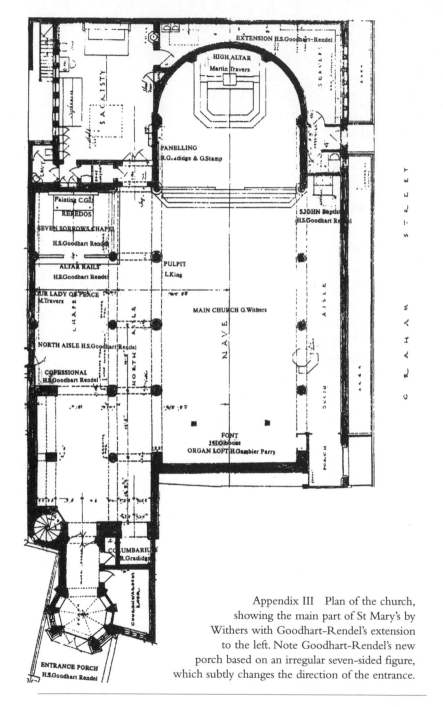

EXTENSION H.S.Goodhart-Rendel

HIGH ALTAR
Martin Travers

SACRISTY

SERVERY

LAVY

PANELLING
R.G.adidge & G.Stamp

Painting C.Gill
REREDOS
SEVEN SORROWS CHAPEL
H.S.Goodhart Rendel

S.JOHN Baptist
H.S.Goodhart Rendel

ALTAR RAILS
H.S.Goodhart Rendel

PULPIT
L.King

OUR LADY OF PEACE
M.Travers

CHAPEL

MAIN CHURCH G.Withers

NORTH AISLE H.S.Goodhart Rendel

NAVE

NORTH AISLE

AISLE

CONFESSIONAL
H.S.Goodhart Rendel

PORCH

FONT
J.H.Gibbons
ORGAN LOFT H.Gambier Parry

COLUMBARIUM
R.Gradidge

G R A H A M   S T R E E T

ENTRANCE PORCH
H.S.Goodhart Rendel

Appendix III   Plan of the church,
showing the main part of St Mary's by
Withers with Goodhart-Rendel's extension
to the left. Note Goodhart-Rendel's new
porch based on an irregular seven-sided figure,
which subtly changes the direction of the entrance.

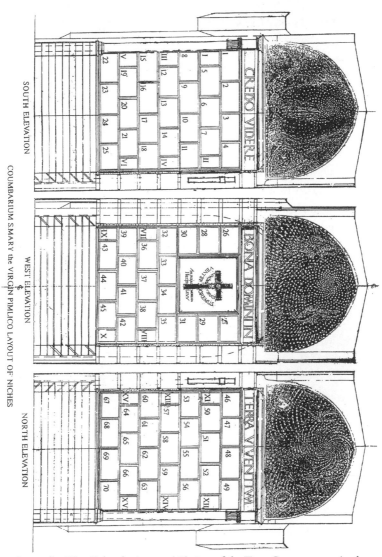

Appendix IV   Columbarium and Shrine of the True Cross: perspective by
Roderick Gradidge 1998. This Columbarium for the ashes of the faithful,
designed by Roderick Gradidge and built by Bill Stainthorpe in a small
vaulted chapel by the Bourne Street entrance. It has painted panels
representing the three resurrections by Anthony Ballantine with the
vault powdered with stars by Christopher Boulter. The splendid
reliquary of the True Cross, itself in the shape of a cross, is by Omar
Ramsden with an engraved glass panel in front by Josephine Harris.

# Church Officers

*Parish Priest*
Fr Bill Scott

*Assistant Priest*
Fr Nick Mercer

*Honorary Assistant Priests*
Canon Lord Pilkington
Fr Stephen Young
Fr Stuart Leamy

*Churchwardens*
Neville Price
Christopher Batchelor

*Treasurer to the PCC*
Krzysztof Romanski

*Secretary to the PCC*
David Richards

*Lay Administrator and Verger*
John Greenhalgh

*Sacristan*
Anne Mundy

*Master of Music*
Shane Fletcher

*Electoral Roll Officer*
Elizabeth Russell

# Contributors

Timothy Ashurst is a former parishioner of St Mary's.

Shane Fletcher is Master of Music at St Mary's.

Roderick Gradidge is an architect and writer.

John Greenhalgh is Verger and Lay Administrator.

Henry Hely-Hutchinson is a former Churchwarden of St Mary's.

David Marchese is Managing Trustee of St Mary's Trust
and a chorister.

Brian O'Brien is a former Managing Trustee of St Mary's Trust
and a former Churchwarden.

Fr David Powell was an Assistant Priest at St Mary's
during the 1930s.

Fr Bill Scott is present Parish Priest at St Mary's.

Fr Stephen Young is Chaplain at St Paul's School in Barnes
and Assistant Priest at St Mary's.

# Acknowledgements

The editor and publisher would like to thank Audrey Stallard and Paul Davis & Partners for the cover photograph; Alan Godfrey Maps for an extract from the *Old Ordnance Survey Map* of 1894; the Royal Institute of British Architects (Drawings Collection); Nicolette Hallet for photographs; Mrs McCall for permission to reproduce her late husband's painting; Helen Armstrong Harvey and Dave Walker from the Royal Borough of Kensington and Chelsea reference libraries; John Sargent from Westminster City Libraries Archives; Michael Boag, Cicely Paget Bowman, Fr John Gilling, Henry Hely-Hutchinson, David Marchese, Brian O'Brien, Glynn Payne, Lisa and Robert Proctor, Ian Rhodes, John Rogers, Kris Romanski, Elizabeth Russell, Nigel Seed, Rodney Warrener for making their advice and experience available; Richard Poole for designing the cover, and Paul Chown for professional advice.